REASONABLE
PLEASURES

Father James V. Schall, SJ

REASONABLE PLEASURES

The Strange Coherences of Catholicism

IGNATIUS PRESS   SAN FRANCISCO

Cover photograph and design
by John Herreid

© 2013 by Ignatius Press, San Francisco
All rights reserved
ISBN 978-1-58617-787-4
Library of Congress Control Number 2013930747
Printed in the United States of America ∞

For if the gods pay some attention to human beings, as they seem to, *it would be reasonable for them to take pleasure* in what is best and most akin to them, namely understanding; and reasonable for them to benefit in return those who most of all like and honor understanding, on the assumption that these people attend to what is beloved by the gods, and act correctly and finely.

—Aristotle, *Ethics*[1]

If I am asked, as a purely intellectual question, why I believe in Christianity, I can only answer, "For the same reason that an intelligent agnostic disbelieves in Christianity." I believe in it quite rationally upon the evidence. But the evidence in my case, as in that of the intelligent agnostic, is not really in this or that alleged demonstration; it is in an enormous accumulation of small but unanimous facts. The secularist is not to be blamed because his objections to Christianity are miscellaneous and even scrappy; it is precisely such scrappy evidence that does convince the mind. I mean that a man may well be less convinced of a philosophy from four books, than from one book, one battle, one landscape, and one old friend.

—G. K. Chesterton, *Orthodoxy*[2]

Thus in the modern world, the celibacy of the medieval learned class has been replaced by a celibacy of the intellect which is divorced from the concrete contemplation of the complete facts.

—Alfred North Whitehead, *Science in the Modern World*[3]

[1] Aristotle, *Nicomachean Ethics*, trans. Terence Irwin (Indianapolis: Hackett, 1985), 1179a25–30 (emphasis added).

[2] G. K. Chesterton, *Orthodoxy* (1908; Garden City, N.Y.: Doubleday Image, 1959), 143.

[3] Alfred North Whitehead, *Science in the Modern World* (New York: Mentor, 1925), 196.

Though the Incarnation of Christ is displeasing to the proud, yet there are also many other *things in it which will prove profitable* for us to examine and to study. One of them is that it has been shown to man what place he would occupy in the things that God has established, seeing that human nature could be so united with God as to become one person from two substances; and, therefore, He is now made up of three: God, the soul, and the flesh.

—Augustine, *On the Trinity*[4]

It were to be wished that they who devote their lives to study would at once believe nothing too great for their attainment, and consider nothing as too little of their regard; that they would extend their notice alike to science and to life, and unite some knowledge of the present world to their acquaintance with past ages and remote events. Nothing has so much exposed men of learning to contempt and ridicule as their ignorance of things which are known to all but themselves.

—Samuel Johnson, *The Rambler*[5]

The perfection of the whole of corporeal nature depends in a certain sense on the perfection of man.

—Thomas Aquinas, *Compendium of Theology*[6]

[4] Augustine, *On the Trinity*, bks. 8–15, trans. Stephen McKenna, ed. Garth B. Matthews (Cambridge: Cambridge University Press, 2002), 13, 17, p. 129 (emphasis added).
[5] Samuel Johnson, *The Rambler* 117 (July 9, 1751): 223–24.
[6] Thomas Aquinas, *Compendium of Theology*, 1.148.

CONTENTS

ACKNOWLEDGMENTS

Chapter 1, "Dogma: What Is It?", was originally published in the *Homiletic and Pastoral Review*, May 2006. The author wishes to acknowledge the publisher for permission to reprint it here.

INTRODUCTION

ON WHAT PROVES PROFITABLE
TO EXAMINE

However, we should examine the origin not only from the conclusion and premise [of a deductive argument], but also from what is said about it; for all the facts harmonize with a true account, whereas the truth soon clashes with a false one.

— Aristotle, *Ethics*[1]

I

The beginning of this book contains six brief citations. Each is worth considerable refection. To be able to "quote", to state again what was first said by someone not of our time and place, to ponder it, and to reflect on it—these are marvelous human capacities. We can know more than we know because someone else already knows and has recorded what he knows. And we can understand what is handed down to us. Each above passage, I think, contributes something essential to what this short book is about.

The title of this book, *Reasonable Pleasures*, comes, in spirit at least, from Aristotle, though not without a hint of pleasures

[1] Aristotle, *Nicomachean Ethics*, trans. Terence Irwin (Indianapolis: Hackett, 1985), 1098b12–13.

and reasons from more specific sources than he knew. Aristotle, no doubt, did most to teach us that knowing itself is a unique pleasure, unlike any others. If we do not experience it, he thought, we likely shall seek other pleasures, usually less noble, to substitute for it. But mainly he guided us to the pleasures of thinking, which includes thinking what is true, the thinking about *all that is*.

Aristotle taught that every activity that is normal to us, including thinking, has its own proper pleasure. This pleasure was not accidental but was designed to enhance, make right, that action in which the pleasure existed. Pleasure was never itself the end of any action but its "bloom" or perfection. If we had the action wrong, the pleasure would still exist, but, with the act itself, it would be deflected away from its proper object.

A human being is free to make such distortions, to misuse pleasure, at every step of his life. This possibility is why, Aristotle thought, both actions and pleasures should be guided by reason oriented to *what is*. The "reasonable pleasure" of this book, as I see it, is the delight we take in knowing the truth of things, especially the truth about ourselves and our place in the existence of things.

"There are things and we know them" is how the French philosopher Étienne Gilson once put the first intellectual affirmation that we must implicitly make before we can state anything else. If we doubt either of these, either that there are things or that we know them, we cannot get out of ourselves. Nothing is clearer than these statements and what they stand for. They are "first principles", evident. Nothing can be and not be at the same time. A thing cannot be true and false at the same time and in the same manner. We must distinguish. This distinguishing is why we have minds.

Nothing can "prove" such immediate principles because nothing is clearer. To deny them is to affirm them. Their denial, at one point or another, leads to the construction of alternate worlds from the one *that is*. Whatever first principles we select, we seek to explain everything else in their light. Most thought and most living include conflicts about reality and how we know it. Much is at stake, including what we are about in this world. We also wonder whether, in our doings and thinking, we also transcend the world we know.

Many people disdain citing Aristotle because, they say, he is unscriptural, or out of date, or illogical. The fact is that he is ever pertinent. He helps make intelligible what is found in Scripture. Indeed, both sources, reason and Scripture, often say the same thing. He possessed the most logical mind we have ever seen. To cite Aristotle is always a pleasure. He was a man of truth. The important truths that he did not know, those dealing with revelation or later science, almost always, as Aquinas understood him, found some initial basis in his thought. Aristotle was like his teacher, Plato, in that when he was wrong, he was always very close to what was right.

The subtitle of this book, *The Strange Coherences of Catholicism*, does not come from anybody in particular, but its overtones are Chestertonian. Chesterton was the great mind who delighted in spelling out all the erroneous, vicious, confused, and silly views about Christianity and Catholicism that he came across in his time in the daily press or culture.[2] Not surprisingly, such odd views, when sorted out, reflected the things that were always wrong whenever or

[2] See James V. Schall, "G. K. Chesterton, Journalist", in *Schall on Chesterton* (Washington, D.C.: Catholic University of America Press, 2000), 1–20;

wherever they appeared. He enjoyed this endeavor because he could see both why the view was proposed and why it was not complete or valid. Humor was also found in the effort. Though laughter may not be the final definition of happiness, surely it includes it. We laugh when we see the point. That too is what this book is about.

Humor arises because we are rational beings who can and do delight in the things that we know, in the things of the mind. We are amused in the comparisons we make, either in speech or in reality, between what we expect and what is said or what happens. The correction of mind by mind is one of the greatest of human enterprises. We do not want, as Plato said, a lie in our souls about the *things that are*. In things of the intellect too, a brother is helped by a brother. Indeed, this correction is one of the great divine enterprises. God, in revelation, undertook to do so Himself.

We live in an era of relativism and skepticism, I know. But we need not accept them as if they were true. We remain free to delight in the fact that the arguments for these and other "isms" never quite cohere, though we need to make the effort to see just why. We are glad to escape the dismal world that follows in the wake of their supposed truth, a wake that Chesterton delighted in following. Ideologies and other deviations from *what is* are seldom amusing, except when we compare them to the truth.

In the tradition of Aquinas, about whom he wrote a wonderful book, Chesterton saw that the doctrines, the morals, and the life of grace do fit together, even though it takes work, virtue, and often some wit and insight to see how

---

Aidan Nichols, *G. K. Chesterton, Theologian* (Manchester, N.H.: Second Spring, 2009).

they do. Chesterton tells us that he spent his early life study-ing the "heretics", not the Christians, whom he never read. Finally, when he noticed that the heretics contradicted each other about the attributes of Christianity, he began to won-der if everything did not after all cohere.

Chesterton understood that such a realization was a strange experience. He knew that truth is one in all its expressions. Even error points to truth if we would but see it. When-ever a strong case was made disproving this coherence, it turned out, on examination, that the case was at some point flawed and could be seen as such. The argument of the heretics, of whatever kind, always has a point. This is why they are worth studying. But the same point can always be made in a more logical and clear way without the error. To see this, we have minds.

Here, I will not argue that, if one is "reasonable", he can pass from knowing the tiniest thing to knowing the Beatific Vision in a few logical steps. That view itself would be, yes, heretical. It would imply that the human mind by itself could not only reach but comprehend the divinity itself. To do this, it would already have to be a divine mind, and each of us knows already, in reflecting on himself, that it is not. It goes without saying that some philosophers claim, implicitly at least, to have such a "divine" mind. They are usually treated under the category of pride, the capital vice in which we locate the center of the universe in ourselves. In reading them, we always come to a point where some-thing does not fit, does not follow.

The classic Catholic praise of mind is also aware of its limits. This very awareness, in fact, is what keeps it open to any intelligence more comprehensive than its own. Yet the Beatific Vision or any transcendent truth, once it has been revealed to us, becomes a reason to think what it might

mean, even though, at first, it might seem impossible or
contradictory. The much-controverted term "Christian philosophy", if it means anything, means that, in seeking to
understand the truths of revelation, we use our minds in
such a way that we discover things the philosophers
overlooked in philosophy itself. We also mean that the truths
of philosophy are reaffirmed in revelation as valid themselves as philosophically based positions.[3]

Human intelligence remains human even when it con-
siders divine things. That too is in Aristotle, as it is in Aquinas. The human mind is capable of being all things—that
is, of knowing all things. But to know anything, it first
needs things. It does not create the things it knows except
in art and craft. Even in these areas, it must presuppose
things and experiences that it did not itself undergo. Such
considerations always return us to the subject of creation.
The world as it is always is more intelligible on the suppo-
sition of a Creator. Those who deny this fact usually end
up thinking themselves the only creators.

II

In this introduction, let me take a further look at each of
the six citations found at the beginning of this book. They
catch the flavor of what I have in mind in this book. I
seek to combine a sense of grandeur about the scope of
what is with humility about what we as individual persons
know. But this humility is not a skepticism about our

[3] See Peter Kreeft, *The Philosophy of Jesus* (South Bend, Ind.: St. Augustine's Press, 2007).

knowing powers as such or an attempt to downplay the centrality of knowing in our own lives. We find an eagerness and liveliness in our hearts about the meaning of everything, beginning with ourselves. We look for guides, for what is addressed to us. If Aristotle is right, all knowledge is addressed to us if we learn how to receive it. In the beginning, each of us is in the strange position of having a mind but with nothing in it. That fact alone should make us realize that mind is not initially a human invention, even if it can reflect on and study itself in retrospect to its being already there knowing things not itself.

Let me begin with the famous passage in Aristotle's *Ethics* about the gods paying "some attention" to human beings. They "seem" to, Aristotle thought. The gods would certainly look to what is best in us, our "understanding". It seems right that they would give us the gift of happiness, if they could, as Aristotle mentions in the passage that begins this introduction. Moreover, it would be "reasonable" for them—Aristotle is thinking of the implications of what he wrote—to be pleased with those of our kind most like the gods. Since the highest thing is pure spirit or reason, it seems reasonable that some people should strive to be like the gods, that is, to use their reason. And they should live their lives according to it; they should act "correctly and finely". This passage is reminiscent of Socrates, of course. Aristotle clearly thinks that by the use of our minds, we can figure many things out that reflect the same "reason" that is found in the gods.

What I conclude from this brief passage in Aristotle, still aware of his vast scope, is that the highest things are related in such a fashion that the benevolence of the gods, if it were to be given to men, would concern what is best for them. On men's part, moreover, they would strive to use this power well, knowing that it can be used badly. Aristotle here combines knowing and acting both "correctly" and "finely". I take these words to mean that acting finely or nobly includes a perfection of reason. This perfection pleases the gods, as it pleases us. Thus, "if the gods pay some attention to human beings", Aristotle says—unlike we Christians, he is not sure that they do—"it would be reasonable for them to take pleasure in what is best and most akin to them, namely understanding."

So I, as a Catholic, read this philosophical, nonrevelational source. I say it is, in its way, exactly right. This Greek philosopher stands within the framework of what makes sense. Now, Aristotle's god is often said to have nothing to do with us except, as a final cause, to be the source of motion, especially intelligible motion. Aristotle's "if the gods pay some attention to human beings", nonetheless, anticipates my understanding of revelation—not just that the gods pay attention to us, but that which pays attention is itself *Logos*, truth, reason. We shall see more of this remarkable relationship.

III

The second passage is from Chesterton. It is the longest passage of the six. Here Chesterton tells us how he responds when someone asks him why he believes in Christianity. He refined this subject to Catholicism in two books after his conversion some fifteen years after he wrote *Orthodoxy* in 1908. Chesterton speaks of a "purely intellectual question". To answer the question, Chesterton compares the same type of question addressed to an "intelligent agnostic". Both, he thinks, believe in their position because of the evidence that they have for their position. Both are "quite rational" in doing so.

Chesterton then adds something quite profound. It is a theme that shall recur in my thoughts in this book. It is that we human beings are more than pure minds, though we have minds. We are beings plunged through our bodies into nature and history, into a world, into time. To believe in Christianity is not primarily a conclusion from a syllogism, though Catholics who read Aristotle are very fond of syllogisms and rightly so. Syllogisms are not to be neglected. But Chesterton said that he is a Christian because of the "enormous accumulation of small but unanimous facts". If the "secularist" blames Christians, he says that their evidence is "miscellaneous", more like a scrapbook collection than an organized argument. To this powerful objection, Chesterton simply agrees while noting that the secularist himself does the same thing.

"It is precisely such scrappy evidence that does convince the mind", Chesterton unexpectedly concludes. A given man may not be convinced of the truth of Christianity by reading Aristotle's logic—though, curiously, another man may be convinced by reading it, one who is surprised that there is a logic to things in the first place. But "four books" of philosophy may not convince us.

Again, things fit together in many ways. The suffering of a child may convince us, just as much as it makes an agnostic of another. This reasoning of Chesterton is really remarkable and true to life, which is broader than mind but includes it. A given "four books" of philosophy may not convince us, but four other books of philosophy may well do so. It depends on the books and what we see there. And, of course, the acceptance of the truth of things also depends on something more—we Catholics call it grace. Our lives are adventures that include these "one book, one battle, one landscape and one friend" scraps of evidence that indicate that things do make sense.

IV

The third citation is from the scientist Alfred North White-head in his famous book *Science in the Modern World*. I cite this passage partly because it has Platonic overtones. My life seems full of Platonic overtones. No one teaches quite so charm-ingly as does Plato, or quite so much. Few students, I have learned, can read Plato halfheartedly, with cold souls. I cer-tainly cannot. Whitehead's sentence actually mirrors the pas-sage of Chesterton that we just considered. Whitehead compares sophisticated scientists in the "modern world" with the "medi-eval learned class". He clearly conceives them both doing the same thing in society but in a radically different mode.

The celibacy of medieval monks stemmed in part from Scripture, from Christ's telling the rich young man to go, sell what he has, and follow Him. But from another angle, the monastic life was the Christian answer to Plato's "guard-ians", who also gave up wives, children, and property.[4] The "celibacy" to which Whitehead referred implicitly includes the other two vows of poverty and obedience. The Pla-tonic guardians were freed from these obligations so that they could identify with the good of the city.

A monk's vows were designed to free the monk to accom-plish things that required lifetime commitment to some

---

[4] See James V. Schall, "The Christian Guardians", *Downside Review* 97 (January 1979): 1–9.

purpose of worship, mind, charity, or service. These vows were not designed for those who lived normal lives in family, with wealth and goods. Such people participated in their own rule of self, household, and polity. The monastic life, the family life, and political life were not seen as opposed to each other but as complementary. All were good, all were needed, all were noble—but all were different.

Whitehead's point concerns modern science and thought. It is all abstract, constructionist in spirit. If one reads Descartes on science, it is as if we can project the world from our own heads. Whitehead's point is that "the concrete contemplation of the complete facts" must take us back to things so that we can see, taste, and understand what they really are. When we "divorce" our minds from attention to real things that we did not make, when we form abstract ideas about them, we begin to live in a "chaste" world that is sufficient unto itself. It was this "celibacy of the intellect" that Whitehead warned us about. The celibacy of the monk was designed so that he could see things, including God, more clearly. It was not a withdrawal from the world based on the idea that the world is unimportant. Rather, the monk's celibacy is an attention to things that are most important, which includes the "concrete contemplation" of all things in its scope.

V

The fourth citation is from Augustine's book on the Trinity. This teaching about the nature of the Godhead is what is central to Christianity, its most glorious contribution

to what God is. Augustine begins by telling us that the
Incarnation is the doctrine and reality that one of the Persons of the Trinity, the Son, became man. Why is this teaching "displeasing" to the proud? Probably because it is the
clearest proof that we ourselves are not gods. We stand in
relation to God not as makers of the highest things but as
receivers of them, of what is good for us beyond our own
imagining. The drama of human existence seems, in fact,
to circle around this question: Are we gods, or are we made
by God? In a basic sense, each human life is spent answer-
ing this question in word and deed.

Augustine adds, however, that this Incarnation will prove
"profitable" to us in many unsuspected ways. We are to
think about what the Incarnation means. We are to "examine and to study" these things at our leisure. One of the
things we can learn, Augustine tells us, is that we can begin
to see our place among the things that God has established.
Why does the Incarnation of the Word teach us this? If we
seek to know what we are, as we can hardly avoid doing,
we must be astonished to learn that "human nature could
be ... united with God." Augustine adds that human nature
is so united with God in the Incarnation that one divine
Person has two substances or natures—one divine, one
human.

This Person, Christ, at the same time, is God; He likewise has a soul and a body, all united in one being, with
what is human still really human and what is divine in Him
really divine. Even though Christ "empties Himself out" to
come among us, as Saint Paul said (cf. Phil 2:7), what was
really happening is that human nature, and all those belonging to it, were elevated to be able to live the divine life that
was not simply human but was the life intended for us by
God in the first place.

VI

The fifth citation is from Samuel Johnson, the great English philosopher and lexicographer. Among us human beings, Johnson was a wise man. He begins with a wish. He speaks of those "who devote their lives to study". He is speaking of the learned, of the academy, of the scientist, to those most apt to be proud. He is already saying that they, in their zeal for abstract theories and systems, neglect to see what Chesterton had called the "one book, one battle, one landscape, and one old friend".

Johnson makes the same point in another way. Nothing is too little for our regard. Even the tiniest things teach us. Both knowledge and life need to be in our attention. Again, we are more than our minds, but we still have minds. We need to know "past ages and remote events". Why? Because they too belong to the same reality as we do. The things that occur in history recount not theories but the lives and deeds of real human beings. This concreteness reminds us that Christianity is not a theory or a series of doctrines. It is first an event that occurred in history among men. The Incarnation is a reflexive understanding of this event, in which many levels of reality were present. The event happened, the birth of a Child, in a certain time and place. The Child came first. The theories followed. All theories always must return to this fact and the subsequent life of this Child.

The learned, Johnson tells us, with some amusement, often display "ignorance of things which are known to all but themselves". That is a marvelous observation. It takes us back to the proud. It brings to mind Plato's Thracian maidens, who laughed at the philosopher who, speaking of exalted things as he walked along, did not notice the hole in the road and fell in. This passage too recalls Chesterton's "common man", who often sees real things to which the learned and mighty are blind.

Without denying the importance of study and learning, if we are going to defend mind, we have to defend it in everyone. We are all capable of the truth. The Incarnation happened apparently in a very obscure place, in a remote part of the world. But this has nothing to do with its central significance. We can say of it, in the words of Whitehead, that we owe it the "concrete contemplation of the complete facts". As Chesterton said, the reason he accepts Christianity as true is the same reason that the agnostic accepts his own theory as true, namely, "the evidence", the facts.

VII

The final passage is very brief, very succinct, as Aquinas is wont to be. Yet, in this single sentence, we have all the distinctions of reality that we most need. The "whole of corporeal nature", the vast cosmos with its curious intelligibility, is not intelligible by its own powers. This limitation, of course, is what is taught in Genesis about the creation. The word *cosmos* means "order". In spite of theories of eternal return and evolution, the cosmos did not "make" itself to be what it is. It did not make its own laws.[5] All the beings in nature follow their own laws, which they did not create themselves.

---

[5] See Stanley Jaki, *The Road of Science and the Ways to God* (Chicago: University of Chicago Press, 1978); Robert Spitzer, *New Proofs for the Existence of God: Contributions of Contemporary Physics and Philosophy* (Grand Rapids, Mich.: Eerdmans, 2010); and William Wallace, *The Modeling of Nature: Philosophy of*

But notice what Aquinas says. He is talking about the "perfection" of this whole cosmos. He says that it does not depend on itself. Or to put it another way, the cosmos exists in order that something else might exist within its domain. The cosmos is not "for itself" as if God created the world as a kind of mechanical toy. But He did create it, from nothing, out of an abundance of His own Trinitarian being and power. In the beginning there was precisely nothing but the fullness of the Godhead. God did not need the universe. He was complete without it. The cosmos is not God. It too points to what is not itself.

Saint Thomas then affirms that the perfection of the cosmos can happen only when the drama of human existence is perfected. The cosmos exists primarily in order than this human drama can happen. We really do not know why such a vast cosmos is needed for our perfection, but we would be foolish to suspect that it is otherwise. This short sentence of Aquinas is the basis of much that will be said in this book. It has its origins really in Trinitarian theology, in what we can figure out about human existence reflecting back on the Incarnation and what it means. The universe is for man, not vice versa. The drama of human life is far more intricate than the complexities of the universe, largely because it also includes our choice, our free will.

I have called this introduction "On What Proves Profitable to Examine". This is a phrase taken from Aristotle, who used it in the context of "What would the gods give us if they could?" The word *profitable* here does not refer to gain or income, though profit is a perfectly legitimate economic factor. Certain events, certain words, certain thoughts

---

Science and Philosophy of Nature in Synthesis (Washington, D.C.: Catholic University of America Press, 1996).

are worth examining. Indeed, when all is done, when economics and politics have done their best, we are still left with the great question of what, after all, it is all about. It is almost as if the gods thought it important that we figure out some things by ourselves. But we have to begin with the facts, including the facts that include revelation.

Christianity includes an understanding of things that exist within the world. But it is also primarily about the life that we lead in view of our understanding. What I want to begin with in the next chapter is some further discussion of the importance and meaning of dogma, or the proper understanding of revelation in the light of what we know with our minds. Christianity includes the proper affirmation and understanding of what is revealed. But it is primarily about a Person, the *Logos*, who is incarnate and who lived among us. In this sense, it is not a thought-to-thought faith but something that seeks, as Saint Paul said, to be face-to-face. And only persons can really be face-to-face.

The perfection of man, as Saint Thomas said, is the reason why the cosmos exists. The human drama has cosmic implications if only to remind us that we need a setting and place wherein we can freely work out what we are intended, invited, to be. The earth, as Genesis says, is given for our use, for our "dominion". Contrary to much ecology theory, which makes the earth an end in itself, our earth becomes more, not less, what it is when we deal with it for our purposes. It has its own beauty and laws, but these are also open to us because we have minds. It is more beautiful because we dwell on it. If we get what is our perfection wrong, we will probably get the world wrong also, even in its physical reality, the reality that makes possible life for the kind of beings we are.

VIII

In conclusion, let me recall the six basic elements in this introduction. They will serve us through the whole of the book. (1) It is reasonable for the gods to take pleasure in what is best and most akin to them. (2) We believe on the basis of evidence, which can be found in books, yes, but also in a battle, a landscape, and in the heart of an old friend. (3) It is easy for the learned to miss the concrete contemplation of everything. (4) The Incarnation proves profitable for us to study and examine because it teaches the elevated place in which we stand in the nature of things. (5) Those who devote their lives to study need to know of life and science. But they also should be aware of what was known in ages past and what is known through remote events.[6] (6) "The perfection of the whole of corporeal nature depends in a certain sense on the perfection of man."

---

[6] A passage from C. S. Lewis' *Screwtape Letters* is worth citing on this point. Screwtape, the demon educator, is advising Wormwood about how to corrupt the learned: "To regard the ancient writer as a possible source of knowledge—to anticipate what he said could possibly modify your thoughts or your behavior—that would be rejected as absolutely simple minded. And since we [devils] cannot deceive the whole of the human race all of the time, it is most important thus to cut every generation off from one another; for where learning makes a free commerce between the ages there is always the danger that the characteristic errors of one may be corrected by the characteristic truths of another." *The Screwtape Letters* (New York: Macmillan, 1961), 129.

CHAPTER 1

DOGMA: WHAT IS IT?*

If the average man is going to be interested in Christ at all,
it is the dogma that will provide the interest. The trouble is
that, in nine cases out of ten, he has never been offered the
dogma.

— Dorothy Sayers, "Creed or Chaos?" [1]

I suppose I have got a dogmatic mind. Anyhow, even when
I did not believe in any of the things called dogmas, I assumed
that people were sorted out into solid groups by the dogmas they believed or disbelieved.

— G. K. Chesterton, *The Autobiography* [2]

I

Let me continue these, as I hope, "reasonable" reflections
with the issue of dogma. What is dogma? Why does it make
any difference what it is? How can its statement be in the
least "relevant", to use a word that itself almost identifies

* This chapter was originally published in *Homiletic and Pastoral Review*
106 (May 2006): 6–12.

[1] Dorothy Sayers, "Creed or Chaos?", in *The Whimsical Christian* (New
York: Macmillan, 1978), 39.

[2] G. K. Chesterton, *The Autobiography* (1936), vol. 16 of *Collected Works*
(San Francisco: Ignatius Press, 1988), 167.

truth with what is going on right now? I confess that I am
a partisan of dogma or doctrine. It is not the only or sole
criterion of what faith holds, to be sure, but it is certainly
one of the criteria. *Dogma* simply means an accurate statement of what is true. Christianity, as I have said, is not a
string of dogmas. It is the life of Christ, who did in fact
live in a certain time and place. He died, was buried, and
rose again. Dogma is the careful effort of the Church to get
it right about this Christ. One slip of a word or an accent
can undermine any statement of truth about Christ; it can
also enervate a civilization or destroy its monuments.

Often the word *dogmatic* has only a pejorative meaning
in the popular mind. Frequently, this effort of the Catholic
Church to state what she holds is said to be what is wrong
with Catholicism. It is too "dogmatic". What is meant by
"formulating dogmas" is that the Church takes a stand and
seeks to state as clearly as possible what is at stake, what she
intends to say, what words mean. Often, people are reluctant to get everything exactly right. The Church cannot
afford not to make this effort to be clear, precise. She has a
vested interest in accuracy even when words change from
one era to another or from one language to another.

To be "dogmatic" means to say the same truth in all ages.
Thus, the believer in the twentieth century holds, in its
essentials, exactly the same thing that someone in the elev-
enth or first century held. Doctrine may "develop", but it
does not change. Indeed, as Blessed John Henry Newman
said, its statements change so that what is held does not
change. We may see deeper implications, or we may understand less well than previous ages, but we see and deal with
the same truth and reality.

Actually, *dogma* is a good word. To speak familiarly of
dogma or doctrine today as an aspect of romanticism will

sound strange to many. We speak familiarly only with persons, especially those we love. With dogmas, we examine
the content of words, their structure, what they say. But, in
a sense, dogma provides the framework of romance. *Romance*
literally means "what they do in Rome". The implication
is that without certain truths held as true, we will all live in
different kinds of world. The world and its loves are held
together by the things affirmed as true. Modern relativism,
by contrast, maintains that the only way we can stick together
is if we deny that anything is true. Unity for the relativist
means a prior agreement that nothing is true.

Yet, when such truths that hold us together are denied, the
world changes; often it falls apart. We cannot expect a man to
be faithful whose philosophy denies that faithfulness is possible in his world. As Samuel Johnson once observed, if we
dine with a man who denies that theft is unjust, the first thing
we should do when he leaves is count the silver spoons. Our
very minds are made with the capacity to affirm that these
things are or are not true. Indeed, our lives are taken up with
such affirmations and denials. We distinguish; we examine;
we see. The "sight" of the mind, its light, is truth.

Contrary to popular assumptions, the terms *dogma* and
doctrine are not intrinsically bad or evil words. No doubt,
they can, in popular parlance, stand for a rigidity in which
careful consideration or reconsideration of an argument, a
term, or a truth is rejected. The motive of this refusal is
often in not frankly admitting that problems concerning
the presentation or meaning of a subject are at issue. But
essentially, a dogma is intended to clarify, to state accurately, to illuminate what can be stated about an experience, an ultimate issue, or something connected to it.

The dogma is not a substitute for the experience or fact
with which it is concerned. We long to behold reality in

itself, to see God face-to-face and know that we do. But we also long to understand, to make sense of what it is that we behold or hold in faith and in observation. Such desire is also intrinsic to the kind of being we are. Dogmas are designed to help in the achievement of these latter objectives. The dogma of the Immaculate Conception is not the Immaculate Conception itself. Rather, it is a careful and accurate way of stating what is meant by this event. The truth of the dogma lies in someone actually knowing what it means, in affirming that it is true by seeing how it relates to what it refers to. In different modes, the being in the mind and the being in things are the same being.

The world of reality and the world of mind are parallel to each other, but the latter depends on the former for its truth, not vice versa. But in a voluntarist world that makes reality depend on changeable will, which is the underlying assumption of much modern or Islamic thought, the mind finds nothing solid to conform to in reality. All is immediately changeable and could be otherwise than it currently is. Everything lacks a stable nature and reality. Truth, as Aquinas said, however, is the conformity of the mind with *what is*, not the opposite; truth is not, except in the case of art, the conformity of reality with whatever the mind wants to be and to be true. We are not makers of reality, of *what is*. We are receivers of it. This principle includes the reality that each of us *is*.

The statement, the word, the affirmation or negation, of what dogma is about and the object that it defines by this statement are not contradictory to each other. The world can and does include both. If they were contradictory, we could know nothing about anything, which is the fate of much modern relativism and skepticism, now conceived as a liberty from "dogma". On this voluntarist hypothesis, our minds and the world would never meet or check one another. The latter, the dogma, depends on the former, on *what is*. The *what-is-to-be-known* always stands for us human beings as prior to and as the basis of our statement of what is known.

A dogma is simply stating accurately, in the best way we can, in the language we know or learn, what we know. No words that state reality are the reality itself that is stated. But the statement does indicate what the reality is that we speak of. The words mean something. That is why there are so many of them. The mind, as Chesterton said, is a "dogma-making" faculty. To deny the mind this capacity to formulate and state what it knows is to deny what it is to be mind in the first place. We are the rational animals, the mortal beings in the universe. We both exist as complete wholes in ourselves and know what is not ourselves, what is out there.

In more recent times, a curious fear has emerged. This is the shock that the dogmas of Catholicism might indeed prove to be true. Thus, what have come to be challenged are not so much the dogmas themselves, in their articulated intelligibility, but the mind's very power to know anything at all, including dogma. If Catholicism does make coherent sense, this attack on the mind itself is a preemptive strike, a final fallback position. Skepticism about our knowing anything, I think, is not unrelated to the suspicion that, in fact, the dogmas might be true.

Therefore, to obviate any possibility of a truth of things, especially of human things, that man did not give to himself, we propose, as a first-line defense, that we can know nothing but what we formulate for ourselves. As a consequence, we are obliged by nothing in being. We are guaranteed "freedom" to do, not what follows from the objective order of things, including human things, but what we want, whatever we choose. No objective "given-ness" can correct us. For nothing objective can be known. To protect ourselves from truth, we are willing to deny the reality that grounds the possibility of ourselves knowing it and hence following it.

This denial of any relation between mind and things generally begins with the epistemological problem, namely, with separating any connection between our senses and our mind. Following a tradition from at least Locke, if not Epicurus, we are said to know only an "image" or a "representation" of reality, not reality itself. But, in fact, what we know through our sensory powers is not a picture or image but the thing itself.[3] We know this reality through the normal and coordinate workings of our senses and our mind as they relate to each other in an orderly fashion. We do not know the images but the thing through our sensory and intellectual powers with their relation to each other.

If we know only the image of a thing, we can never know anything outside of ourselves, including one another. And, of course, if we cannot know what is not ourselves, we cannot even know ourselves. The knowledge we have of ourselves comes initially and indirectly through our knowing what is not ourselves. We know ourselves not directly but indirectly through knowing what is not ourselves. I know myself reflectively because it is I who know something else. The very knowledge of ourselves is a gift from what is not ourselves. Ultimately, this hints that all things are finally gifts.

[3] The best book on this whole subject of knowing is Robert Sokolowski, *The Phenomenology of the Human Person* (New York: Cambridge University Press, 2008).

Not infrequently, moreover, we find that the effort to articulate dogmas, itself often a classically "Catholic" endeavor, is under attack because, it is held, human beings substitute or confuse the statement of the dogma or doctrine with the reality itself to which the dogma points. Thus, it is held, we believe in dogmas but not that toward which dogmas direct us or what they articulate. Catholics, for instance, consciously and deliberately say the Creed, which is a string of dogmas, together at Sunday Mass.

At bottom, the Church recognizes that Catholicism is an intellectual faith. Its members know and want to know precisely what it is that they hold about the Trinity and its Persons in relation to us. The Creed is the minimal but most accurate statement of this "holding" insofar as it can be properly formulated by the human mind considering revelation and what it means. It is always theoretically possible to improve the statement of the dogma, make it more precise. But improvement, if it occurs, depends on evidence and does not obviate the truth of the dogma in its previous form.

When we say this Nicene Creed, the objection goes, we are said to believe in the Creed as a statement but not in that to which the Creed points. As a matter of fact, I doubt whether few, if any, believing Catholics actually make this subtle distinction, however much they are accused of it for being "dogmatists". But if, in spite of it all, they should do so, it would prove that they do not believe in a reality but only in a statement of reality. While this confusion is possible, the accusation, I think, is often an effort to prevent us from making the effort to state what the doctrine actually indicates. It is the perfection of our minds to know the truth of a thing in all its available forms. We are driven to know things and make proper statements about them, the same things.

Thus, it is a perfection of the human mind to state, however imperfectly, though as accurately as possible, what reality means through the formulation of a stated dogma. Nowhere in Catholic tradition is it claimed that the dogma or doctrine as a statement is, even by reason of its accuracy, something that exhausts or substitutes for the actual reality of what is defined. Nor is it claimed that no better statement can ever be concocted. This better statement depends on facts and genius of expression. The dogma is always designed to encourage us to pursue a further knowledge, understanding, and, indeed, love of the *what is* that we seek to know. A dogma points to the reality that it formulates.

II

Catholicism has always taken dogmatic statements seriously because it realizes that failure to state the truth properly can lead, and often does lead, to error and confusion. Wars and hatred have no doubt been related to this problem of the accurate statement of the truths of things. Historical relations with Orthodoxy, with Islam, with Protestantism, with Marxism, with modern liberalism, with other religions are at bottom rooted in theological questions having to do with the proper understanding of reality—of God, man, and the cosmos.

This conflict or disagreement about the highest things and their proper statement, however, is also one of the sources of skepticism about dogmas. Dogmas are said to cause wars; dogmatic disagreements are seen as mere quibbles over nothing important. The argument presumably follows that, if we forbid or deny doctrine, prevent or hinder its public expression, we will have peace. If we agree, however, that nothing is true, we will, it is said, be free from all the fanaticism of the dogmatists, or so it is claimed.

In another sense, this controversy or turmoil surrounding dogmatic statements, while we do not easily praise it, does witness to the long-range importance of getting things right in our understanding of them. Things, both divine and human things, really are at stake if we misunderstand the meaning of dogmas. Many a beautiful statue or building has been destroyed by an iconoclastic dogma holding that any representation of the divine is evil. Nor does it follow that because a dogma is true it will be accepted by those who do not see its truth. Dogmas are not efficacious without the will also to accept and understand them.

Nothing in revelation, however, gives us cause for thinking that its proper understanding and statement make no difference to us or to the world. The "going forth and teaching" all nations (cf. Mt 28:19) means at least this, that lacking proper dogmas, lacking the proper understanding of ultimate things, is a detriment to every people. The famous Aristotelian dictum, that "a small error in the beginning leads to a greater error in the end", moreover, has its validity and, indeed, its history. The idea that no dogma is true is itself a dogma. And if it is this "dogma" that claims itself to be true, it contradicts itself in its very statement. So the effort to find the truth of dogmas is in fact unavoidable if we wish to be sane about what the world and our relationship to it means.

The term *dogmatic theology*, before its subject matter came to be called the more ambiguous *systematic theology*, used to mean the orderly effort to spell out, in careful philosophic terms, what was revealed to us about God, man, and the world. It was concerned primarily with the truth of what was revealed as presented in clear and orderly terms that we could understand and accept. When anyone reads the various accounts of the life of Christ and the events leading up to His birth, both remotely in the Old Testament and more particularly in the New Testament, questions of exact meaning or understanding were bound to occur to anyone with a minimum of curiosity.

Absolutely nothing is wrong with seeking to examine and resolve any apparent contradictions or seemingly insoluble problems found in the sources of revelation. Indeed, it would be wrong not to seek to do so. Human beings cannot live with the internal suspicion of a contradiction in things, especially in divine things. The famous "two truth" theory, found in Western, Islamic, and other systems, held that a truth of revelation and a truth of reason could and do contradict each other in the same person, yet both still are true. This position is a formula for madness. Such a danger explains why the Church, with Aquinas, doggedly maintained and sought to demonstrate that reason and revelation did not contradict, but supported, each other.

The human mind is a searching instrument or faculty of our souls whereby we are and should be in a constant state of wonderment about anything *that is*. Christ calls God His Father. He does not call Him an "It". He does not call Him a "She" either. Nor does Christ call His Father a "Form", or an "Energy", or some static or dynamic abstraction. Maybe Christ was just confused, though that creates other problems that too must be sorted out. If He was confused, no reason can be found to take Him seriously.

Christ maintained that He and the Father are "one" while also asking the Father to let this "chalice" pass from Him (Jn 10:30; Mt 26:39). It might be all right to hold one or the other of these positions, but both? Surely some inconsistency exists here. With the aid of philosophy, it is the function of theology to spell out, in terms of dogmatic statements, the consistency of what happens or is claimed to happen in revelation whereby both of these affirmations are true and not contradictory.

Revelation is a claim to truth, a truth we are both expected and delighted to know about and accept because we understand its credibility. But the truth is itself a statement of a reality that exists. We are addressed on the grounds of truth in what is revealed. It is not true because it is revealed. It is revealed because it is true. This truth will be coherent with all other truth, including the truths of reason. This position follows Aquinas' principle that "grace builds on nature." Grace does not contradict or overturn nature. This relationship means that we ought to see why they do not contradict each other, or better, why they belong together.

We cannot help but make an effort to state precisely what is to be held as true and, if possible, the reasons for this conclusion. But, then, why would we think that demonstrating that something was inconsistent proved anything wrong with it? Maybe the world is itself incoherent. Maybe anything flows from anything. Perhaps no meaning can be discovered. We just arbitrarily assign meanings as we see fit or as suits our private purposes. Nonetheless, if things are so unconnected and incoherent, why bother to worry about them? The very fact that we bother indicates that their truth still provokes us to find out about it.

What is wrong with suspecting that things fit together? And if they do fit together, we are not wrong to seek to explain why they do (or do not, for that matter). That point brings us to the question: What is an explanation anyhow? An explanation is not necessarily true because everyone believes it, though that common acceptance is an indication that its claim should be taken seriously. Rather, it seems more likely that, if everyone holds something to be true, it is because it is evident to the normal mind that some valid argument can be found for it. Mathematical propositions are famous for their clarity and inner logic. The easier ones are comprehended by almost everyone who takes the trouble to grasp the terms of their proposition and how they are related. No reason exists why other things might not be made clear to most by other intuitions and arguments.

Dogmatic truths, even if they require faith to hold them, nonetheless bear their own inner logic and consistency. They invariably, when examined, betray mind. When carefully examined, they seem to be addressed to enigmas that philosophic truths or arguments do not in fact fully answer, though they approach them and want to know about them. The fact that philosophy, to be philosophy, must remain open to what it does not know, to the love of wisdom, means that, intrinsically, it cannot reject positions addressed to it from whatever source. That would be, well, irrational and a denial of what philosophy is.

How does philosophy know that something in its own order, the order of reason, is addressed to it from the "outside", as it were? The short answer to this question is that certain things are found in revelation that are likewise found in philosophy, as if at least to imply that the same mind lies behind them both. This is particularly the case if the major issues that philosophy does not itself answer also have coherent or sensible answers in revelation to genuine philosophic questions.

III

In his *Philosophical Dictionary*, Mortimer Adler included for examination the word *dogmatism*. He thought that most people fail to see the proper theological sense of the word as "referring to the articles of religious faith", as distinct from philosophical questions, where "dogmatism is totally inappropriate." Philosophical questions as such need to be submitted to "rational inquiry" on which their truth or falsity is based. Still, Adler thought, some philosophical positions can be found, "the affirmation of which are beyond the power of reason to establish". Philosophy, in other words, recognizes its own limits. It suspects its own answers are not complete. With that, it recognizes that it is concerned with a whole that it does not completely grasp, though it seeks to.

As an example of this latter principle of something reason cannot itself establish, Adler uses the instance of "ontological materialism". This rather elevated-sounding position holds that "nothing really exists except bodies and their physical transformations." Using the evidence of logic itself, Adler points out that "that thesis, being a denial, therefore is a negation, and as such it is indemonstrable." That is, we might be able to prove that something is there, or that something is necessary if what is there exists. But the proposition "what is not body does not exist" cannot hold on its initial premise about material bodies.

Simply because we know that bodies exist, we cannot conclude that what is not body does not exist. Obviously, if something that is not body exists, it exists in a nonbodily way. Adler suggests that most scientists inadvertently accept the materialist thesis "without a logical qualm". Evidence of our senses does tell us that material things exist. This is true.

"There is no evidence that reality does not and cannot include the immaterial and the nonphysical. To assert that it does not and cannot is sheer 'dogmatism,' of a kind that should be avoided in philosophy." [4] It is this kind of "dogmatism" that Catholicism seeks to avoid in its own understanding of the meaning of its dogmas, either theological or philosophical.

What, then, is the evidence that what is not physical exists? This alternative is why Plato is always good for us to know. Plato forever stands for the principle that the idea of a thing and the particular existing thing of a certain kind are not exactly the same. The idea or form of a thing is universal. It prescinds from matter. What it is to be a tree may have been acquired from observing many actual trees. But it is not the same as an individual tree, though both have what it is to be a tree in common.

The idea of a tree does not change, ever, even if all actual trees cease to exist. Trees come and go; the idea of a tree, or of a man, does not. We may need minds to think these ideas, but they are not material even when we know that the actual tree before us is largely material. "There is no evidence that reality does not and cannot include the immaterial and the nonphysical." Indeed, in our very minds in their functioning, we reflectively see that something more than what is material is present.

IV

The great encyclical *Fides et Ratio* of Blessed John Paul II was particularly concerned with the philosophical knowledge,

---

[4] Mortimer Adler, *Philosophical Dictionary* (New York: Touchstone, 1995), 88.

or lack thereof, of theologians. It was quite aware that everywhere we look in biblical or theological questions, behind them are also basic philosophical questions that can condition how we understand revelation and the propositions explaining it. The Church has prided herself historically in insisting that she had no "philosophic system" of her own, that she was open to any philosophy provided that it could maintain its truth in the light of philosophy itself.

Yet the Church has, since the Middle Ages, been aware of the presence of Thomas Aquinas, with the idea that not every philosophy is equal simply because it claims to be a philosophy. Indeed, the Church has frankly stated that not every philosophy can sustain or present a coherent understanding of the truths contained within revelation. Not all philosophical systems are true, even though probably a point of truth can be found even in their errors. There are, nonetheless, philosophies, were they consistently held, that would make the Incarnation or the Trinity, the basis truths of Catholicism, impossible of understanding or acceptance. It is at this point where a philosophical system leads to a denial of a truth of revelation that an examination of the validity of any philosophy as philosophy becomes imperative.

Faith is itself directed precisely to intelligence. The Church strives to understand what is revealed in all its perplexity and complexity. As a by-product of this endeavor to understand what is revealed, a deepening of philosophy seems quite likely. This effort also implies a confirmation of that philosophy more capable of explaining the coherent meaning of *what is*. Aquinas states: "What comes from God is well-ordered. Now the order of things consists in this, that things are led to God each one by the others." [5]

---

[5] Thomas Aquinas, *Summa theologiae* I-II, q. 111, a. 1 (my translation).

If we understand the logic of this position, it means that philosophy, by being what it is, is open to or aware of its own limitations. This is not a defect in philosophy but an honest judgment about its own nature. Revelation, on the other hand, by being what it is, leads philosophy and other disciplines and realities to what they are, to knowing more of what they are than they would without the stimulus of revelation. But it does so on the grounds of reason, not revelation.

As I mentioned earlier, in the modern world, philosophy has often deliberately closed itself off from considering anything to do with revelation. We find a fear that things might just cohere. A whole that somehow includes both reason and revelation is possible. The human mind in fact is able to invent numerous reasons for not doing what is right or not accepting what is true. Any human person can choose to follow some path or position of its own formulation as a reason for doing what he wants.

A more sophisticated modern version of this position exists. Philosophy, it is said, is not in principle to be understood as anything but what the human mind can know by its own powers. This methodological limitation, generally called "rationalism", would mean that philosophy must a priori reject any "addition" or "deepening" of itself that would, even if true, come from outside its own control, no matter how "real" or fruitful such an addition was to this same truth.

Philosophic rationalism, on such a thesis, could only reject what was concluded by philosophy's own efforts to understand or articulate what is revealed or to resolve the apparent difficulties or contradictions said to be found in revelation. But we can have a genuine philosophical position derived indirectly from considerations of revelation. In this context, we do not accept the philosophic position because it is gained under the stimulus of revelation. Rather, we accept it because philosophy itself now sees a point it did not see before. We do not reject what is true if it is philosophy but arrived at with the prodding of revelation. It would be unphilosophical to do otherwise.

Thus, the rejection of philosophy derived from the reflection on revelation seems to be itself an unphilosophical act. It refuses even to consider an issue that arises from revelation, whether one believes it or not. A genuine philosophy would mean an openness to a truth, from whatever source. It would wonder about the nature of the revelational reflection that caused deeper philosophic insight. The question comes down to the matter of the alternative: Either we have a genuine openness to *what is* or we have a systematic restriction of philosophy to a rationalism that, contrary to the nature of philosophy itself, sets limits on what it can think.

The meaning of dogma, in conclusion, takes us back to the observation of Dorothy Sayers cited at the beginning of the chapter. The normal person, she remarked, is interested in dogma. He wants to know the truth. It is a "rational pleasure" to know it. But it is rarely presented to him in terms that he can understand. Lacking the proper explanations, many likely go about listening to or concocting ideas that are far from the true understanding of what the faith teaches or what reality is.

Likewise, Chesterton remarks that, even before he realized the intrinsic importance of dogma, he clearly saw that people implicitly organize themselves according to dogmatic ideas or positions. Skepticism itself is such a dogma about which people are known to organize themselves. To understand such ideas, it is necessary to examine what people hold. Chesterton's famous book *Heretics* (1905) was precisely about this point. The real choice is not between dogma and no dogma but between a dogma that is true and one that is not.

In the end, we want to know the truth of things. Yet we often do not want to know the truth if it requires us to change our lives. Yves Simon remarked that for intellectuals and academics in particular, one of the most difficult things they face is the necessity to change their minds when they discover that their favorite theory does not prove to be true.[6] Similarly, Saint Paul wrote to Timothy that many would come to believe in almost any doctrine, however outlandish, once they refused to accept what the faith held to be true and the expressions of it that we call dogmas (see 2 Tim 4:3–5). The alternative to a true dogma is not, in practice, no dogma but a dogma that is not true.

If there is anything peculiar about revelation, it is its insistence that certain truths need to be known if we are to be saved. Faith is also a matter of intelligence. We are to live upright lives on the basis of these truths, to be sure. Revelation does address our intellects with a claim to be true. It is the truth, we are told, that will make us free. Nothing less. We see and articulate the alternatives. Dire things follow when truth is not known or acknowledged. We see such consequences worked out in historical reality, these alternatives to the truth of things as embodied in cultures and nations. We suspect that the effort of revelation to address itself also to our minds about the truth of our being is at the heart of what revelation is about.

Generally speaking, we do not live well if we do not think well. This is why, whatever else it is, Catholicism is

---

[6] See Yves Simon, *A General Theory of Authority* (Notre Dame, Ind.: University of Notre Dame Press, 1980).

an intellectual claim that addresses our minds in the name of what any mind can think. Its dogmas are statements that correspond with reality. We find a pleasure in knowing such truths, and as we will see in the following chapter, we find a certain correspondence between orthodoxy and humor. It was Belloc, I believe, who said, correctly, that "he who has the faith has the fun." That too is a "rational pleasure".

CHAPTER 2

WIT AND HUMOR

A celebrated wit being mentioned, he [Johnson] said, "One may say of him as was said of a French wit, '*Il n'a de l'esprit que contre Dieu.*' I have several times been in company with him, but never perceived any strong powers of wit. He produces a general effect by various means; he has a cheerful countenance and a gay voice. Besides his trade is wit. It would be as wild in him to come into company without merriment, as if a highwayman were to take the road without his pistols.

— *Boswell's Life of Johnson*[1]

If you are a person who looks at the funny side of things, then sometimes when you are the lowest, when everything seems totally hopeless, you will come up with some of your best ideas. Happiness does not create humor. There's nothing funny about being happy. Sadness creates humor.... Charlie Brown has to be the one who suffers, because he is a caricature of the average person. Most of us are much more acquainted with losing than we are with winning. Winning is great, but it isn't funny. While one person is a happy winner, there may be a hundred losers using funny stories to console themselves.

—Charles Schulz, *My Life with Charlie Brown*[2]

[1] James Boswell, *Boswell's Life of Johnson* (London: Oxford University Press, 1931), April 24, 1779, 2:292.
[2] Charles Schulz, *My Life with Charlie Brown*, ed. M. Inge (Jackson: University Press of Mississippi, 2010), 125, 149.

But I who am old will give you advice, which is this—to consider chiefly from now onward those permanent things which are, as it were, the shores of this age and the harbours of our glittering and pleasant but dangerous and wholly changeful sea.

—Hilaire Belloc, *The Four Men*[3]

I

Knowing what a dogma is, that it is an honorable and accurate statement of objective truth, effects in us what I call a "reasonable pleasure". It is comforting to know that reality checks our thoughts and how we formulate and speak them. We do not "make" the world. We live in one already there, not of our own making. But we are beings who want to know in everything we do and experience. We want to state what we know. We constantly strive to articulate in words that others can understand what we encounter in *what is*. Further, when we hear something funny, for instance, we look to tell someone else about it. We are the beings who speak. We speak to one another. We can be amusing and lightsome. Words cannot be addressed only to ourselves as their meaning is intelligible in principle to all. They always bear the fact that they point to others, that they also might understand them.

Saint Paul tells the Corinthians: "Even if I am unskilled in speaking, I am not in knowledge" (2 Cor 11:6). Paul was not as inarticulate as he implies here. But he did know what he was talking about, what he wanted to say with his

---

[3] Hilaire Belloc, *The Four Men: A Farrago*, November 2, 1902 (London: Thomas Nelsen, 1912), 302.

"unskillful speaking". We know more than we can articulate, but this gap is no reason not to come as close to the proper statement of a thing as we can. Paul also said that he "heard things that cannot be told, which man may not utter" (2 Cor 12:4). Reality is larger than our dogmas and our words, but that is because it points to the Word, to the things that we must hear first from outside of ourselves, indeed from outside of our world.

In letters, books, and media we speak or listen to those not present immediately before us. No matter how proud or independent we are, we are not so isolated or so autonomous that we can think of ourselves without also thinking of others. The minute we try to think of ourselves alone, separate from others, we become opaque even to ourselves. We can attend to particular things, to tiny things, as I like to say, but also to the great things, to the highest things.

We are bound in our concrete lives to this time and that place in which we find ourselves. But in our thoughts, we can range anywhere that we can find beings with reason to tell them how they see things or to listen to how they speak them. And the things without reason, the animals, plants, and minerals in the vistas of the world, we confront them too. We name them. They force us to say: "This is not that." We wonder about them; we admire them; we classify and we use them.

To follow a chapter on dogma with a chapter on wit and humor may seem odd, even provocative. In the citation above, Samuel Johnson chides local English wit by referring to similar French wit. Neither of the two witty men mentioned seems to have been genuinely humorous. Such is the meaning of Johnson's citation in French—his spiritual attitude always runs against God. The Frenchman could be "witty" only if he used vulgar or blasphemous language. Such wit reflects a cynical soul bored with reality, not one enchanted with the delight of *things that are*. Genuine wit he seemed to lack. The best of our humor is not *"contre Dieu"*. This fact itself is something to wonder about. The innocent likewise laugh, perhaps most of all.

All the way through human experience and literature, including the Bible, however, we come across instances of laughter that are mocking, bitter, or haughty. In the Second Psalm, the Lord who "sits in the heavens laughs; the LORD has them in derision" (v. 4). Why? It is because "the kings of the earth set themselves, and the rulers take counsel together, against the LORD and his anointed" (v. 2). Such divine laughter, no doubt, is terrible in the ears of the kings and princes with their plottings. A place for derisive laughter, I suppose, can be found when the pretentions of our kind really do claim to rival the divinity, as they do more often than we like to admit. Indeed, all disorders of soul, even the smallest ones, occur when the command of our will replaces what ought objectively to be said or done.

I am mindful of a witticism I once heard: "If you want to make God laugh, just tell him what you are going to do next month." I have heard people cite this passage a surprisingly number of times, almost as if it strikes true in many souls. The fact is: God knows; we do not. In this difference lies the root of our humor, the unexpected disproportion of one thing to another as suddenly seen in one mind, our mind. Quite often, also, the best things in our lives happen because something terrible or painful or sad happened first, without which the joy could never have come to be. Sadness and laughter are paradoxically related.

Though forgiven by sacrament, we are fully restored to normalcy when we can also laugh at our sins. "Laughing till we cry" and "smiling through tears" are common human experiences in which both elements are present. On the whole, we probably find as much, if not more, sadness than laughter in life, even in the lives of wits and saints. We need also to account for this fact. Adam and Eve probably laughed in the Garden, so I do not think that laughter is solely the result of the Fall and its sober aftermath.[4] But scornful or bitter laugher probably is.

This discussion of wit, moreover, has a relation to dogma. Our religious or moral theories can make it impossible, improper, or unlikely for us to laugh. We can laugh only if our conception of the world allows us to do so. It is true that the pessimist or the determinist may still laugh occasionally. The question is whether he is logical in doing so. Does his mental system actually allow it? If I think that no ultimate happiness or joy for man is possible, only this vale of tears and then oblivion, is not all my laughter hollow?

---

[4] C. S. Lewis gives the following "diabolical" analysis of laughter in *The Screwtape Letters*: "I [Screwtape] divide the causes of human laughter into Joy, Fun, the Joke Proper, and Flippancy. You will see the first among friends and loves reunited on the eve of a holiday. Among adults some pretext in the way of Jokes is usually provided, but the facility with which the smallest witticisms produce laughter at such a time shows that they are not the real cause. What that real cause is we [the devils] do not know. Something like it is experienced in much of the detestable art which the humans call Music, and something like it occurs in Heaven—a meaningless acceleration in the rhythm of celestial experience, quite opaque to us. Laughter of this kind does us no good and should always be discouraged. Besides, the phenomenon is of itself disgusting and a direct insult to the realism, dignity, and austerity of Hell. Fun is closely related to Joy—a sort of emotional froth arising from the play instinct. It is very little use to us. . . .

"The Joke Proper, which turns on sudden perception of incongruity, is a much more promising field. . . .

"But flippancy is the best of all. In the first place, it is very economical. Only a clever human can make a real Joke about virtue, or indeed about anything else; any of them can be trained to talk as if virtue were funny." *Screwtape Letters* (New York: Macmillan, 1961), 50–52.

Laughter in itself, I think, is one of the signs of eternal life, a topic to which I shall return in the final chapter.

So I would argue this proposition: That particular philosophical or theological theory is most correct, most likely to be true, which can best account for laughter and joy. Thus, it must also relate them to sadness. Joy and gladness are, however, considerably more difficult to explain than evil, suffering, or unhappiness. The French wit who drew the listeners' attention to himself by blaspheming God revealed his own soul, not God's nature. How is it, after all, that we live in a universe in which, among us, laughter is possible at all? It seems like one of the things that the world could do without, as it "produces" nothing but perhaps more of itself. Laughter, however, belongs to the abundance of things, to the fact that we are given much more than we absolutely need, besides being given also what we do need. We are given *what we are*.

Charlie Brown is sitting on the bench at the edge of the infield. Lucy is about to bat. In his managerial capacity, working out strategy in advance, he tells her: "If you get on base this time, Lucy, see if you can steal second base." Every baseball player understands this basic instruction. However, with her baseball bat in hand and her baseball cap on her head, Lucy turns to him quizzically: "How will I know it's second base? Does it have a number on it? What if I steal ninth base by mistake?"

As Lucy turns to go to the plate, Charlie crosses his eyes in perplexity over such, on the surface, absurd questions. "It's funny", he muses to himself. "That's one of those things a manager never thinks about." [5] It is frustrating to think

<hr>

[5] Charles Schulz, *Being a Dog Is a Full-Time Job* (1944; Kansas City: Andrews and McMeel, 1989), 70.

about them. They imply that Lucy has no clue indicating what the game of baseball is about. Nor does she really care to find out. Since she is needed in the outfield even to have a team, Charlie has to put up with her.

To understand such a scene, one has to know something of baseball. If someone knew the rules only of soccer, he could not see why that Charlie Brown scene was funny. One of the key players does not know what "stealing second base" means. The readers do. The word *steal* has several meanings. It usually means theft, taking something not yours. In baseball, it also has the connotation of safely taking yourself what is not rightfully given by a hit, a fly ball, a walk, or being struck by a pitched ball.

Though he should know better, the manager presumes that the batter, Lucy, understands the terminology. The idea of bases with numbers on them is itself amusing. It shows us the status of Lucy's grasp of the game. Everyone knows that baseball bases themselves do not have painted on them the numbers 1, 2, and 3 and the letter *H*. Of course, it is possible, but not likely, that Lucy also knows this fact but is just playing dumb to provoke Charlie.

The manager strives to put all eventualities on the field under control. "Steal second!" In her own terms, the batter asks a perfectly logical question: "How do I know it's second?" But it is also a silly question, granting that everyone on the field and in the land should know the basic rules and terminology of baseball. Lucy's character is perfectly logical. She's just out there in right field looking at the clouds. Charlie knows that you cannot play baseball if you do not care. Charlie cares. Lucy is logical. We are amused. Such things delight us. "Why?" we wonder. And why are we the kind of beings who can be delighted?

It is in the spirit of a scene like this baseball game in a
Peanuts cartoon that I want to approach the issue of wit
and humor. We begin with the fact that we do laugh,
even if we cannot define or explain the phenomenon.
We know what it is because we do it. Humor lies in
the suddenly appreciated incongruity of it all, in the great
fact that such incongruous and unrelated things do happen to everyone in this life. Our humor reminds us of
our finiteness. The characters of the players, the situation,
and the logical question that has nothing to do with the
game except equivocally—all of these elements need to
be held together in one active mind before the humor will
be manifest. It often comes suddenly. We see that the mistake could have been made over the usage of the verb *to
steal*.

If someone does not know that only three bases are used
in baseball plus home plate, asking how to identify the
second one and how it is different from "ninth base" is
perfectly reasonable. It is our reason that enables us to laugh.
There is no ninth base. I consider this a pleasant reasoning, a dogma, undefined to be sure, but still a dogma. That
the world is full of laughter that is just amusing, delightful, and not blasphemous, scatological, or unkind is almost
the best thing about us. It is something that should hopefully be present in most of the days of our lives, even the
worst.

In retrospect, the funniest things are often those incidents that did not seem funny at the time but are so in
the retelling. Joy and laughter are not the same, but they
are related. Joy is broader than laughter. Joy is the experience of possessing what we know and love. But all laughter, even the mocking kind and the puns, reveal reason at
work.

II

Wit comes from an old English word for knowledge, though, as in the passage from Boswell, it often refers to humor or to one who creates it. "He is a great wit" has come to mean that someone is funny or clever, even a bit off-balance. But it can properly mean someone who sees the amusing incongruities in human affairs. He does not make them up. They are really there. But they need to be pointed out, articulated. Humor and wit exist only when we are actually considering the incongruities and, indeed, appreciating them. Such are among the great blessings of human existence.

In this chapter, I want to say something about the relation of dogma to humor. I want to follow the comment of Charles Schulz that I cited at the beginning. He remarked that it is the sad who laugh most, that it is the losers who, more than we admit, have the best time. Losers too play the game, for without them no game is possible. Philosophic and religious worlds do exist in which laughter is not encouraged, in which it is even punished. No doubt, with Ecclesiastes, there is "a time to weep, and a time to laugh" (Eccles 3:4). There are times to be silent, during which the most amusing things often happen. We then valiantly strive to suppress our laughter. As Aristotle said in the fourth book of his *Ethics*, we cannot laugh all the time at the risk of becoming frivolous buffoons, nor can we refuse to laugh at all at the risk of becoming bores and dullards. Save us from the witless man who laughs at nothing.

In another scene that makes the point clearer, Charlie Brown is on the mound looking at Schroeder in the catcher's mask. Charlie says to him: "We're getting slaughtered again,

Schroeder ... I don't know what to do ... Why do we have to suffer so?" Schroeder replies to Charlie, behind whom, in ball cap, Linus is now standing. Schroeder, in answer to Charlie's question, cites Scripture: "Man is born to trouble as the sparks fly upward!" To this, Charlie can only say: "What?" Linus explains to Charlie: "He's quoting from the Book of Job, Charlie Brown ... seventeenth verse, fifth chapter." The scene is solemnly incongruous yet quite insightful. Charlie's question, in a sense, is answered.

In the next panel, Lucy also comes to the mound. Linus continues to her: "Actually, the problem of suffering is a very profound one ..." Then Schroeder and Lucy get into an argument. Schroeder says to her: "That's what Job's friends told him. But I doubt if ..." Lucy shoots back: "What about Job's wife? I don't think she gets enough credit." Meanwhile, two other members of the team come to the mound. Schroeder says: "I think a person who never suffers, never matures ... Suffering is actually very important."

At this, Lucy shouts: "Who wants to suffer? Don't be ridiculous." Then the other fielder joins in: "But pain is a part of life and ..." Linus continues to an angry Lucy and now also to Snoopy: "A person who speaks only of the 'patience' of Job reveals that he knows very little of the book! Now, the way I see it ..." All of this takes place while the team is supposed to be playing baseball. So Charlie, the pitcher-manager, concludes in some daze: "I don't have a ball team ... I have a theological seminary." [6]

To account for such laughter, we do need theology, I think. Our themes are there in this cartoon: dogma, suffering, pain, patience, and reasoning about them all. Such are profound issues. But the whole scene is amusing and

[6] Charles Schulz, *Peanuts*, United Features Syndicate, 1967.

instructive at the same time. In our laughter, the highest issues can come up: Why do we have to suffer? If the team were winning, such issues probably would not arise. Sadness and laughter again are related. There is something redeeming in the fact that we can and do laugh, eventually even at our sins and failures.

At the end of *Orthodoxy*, Chesterton said that the only thing that the Lord concealed from us when He was on earth was His "mirth"—such a wonderful word! Chesterton thought that if, as Christ did, we beheld the true joy in which the divine life dwells, and for which we are finally created, we would be overwhelmed and depressed by comparison with our present earthly state. Therefore, Christ withheld his mirth. Here on earth, we have but a fleeting capacity to imagine what the ultimate joy is about. Christ is recorded as weeping but not as laughing. And yet the fact of laughter is truly one of the hints indicating what reality is about. Chesterton's point was perhaps more profound than we at first suspect.

In the twentieth chapter of John, the risen Christ appears to Mary Magdalene. He asks her: "Woman, why are you weeping?" (Jn 20:13). She tells Him that it is because they have taken her Lord. Then she recognizes Him, who He is. The weeping ceases. He tells her that He is ascending to His Father. She is to go to tell the brethren. She does. Such is the foundation of our joy, the link between weeping, laughing, and delight. Dogma is what preserves the moment and its real meaning. This preservation is why dogma is stated universally. But he who is present in the moment thinking is greater than the dogma's words stating it. He is not apart from it. "He was crucified, died, and was buried. On the third day, He rose again and ascended into heaven" (Apostles' Creed). We also need to know that Christ did these things.

Chesterton, in a famous passage, recalled being criticized because, in his writing of God and reality, he was also most humorous. Some critics complained that, because he was amusing, he was not a "serious" thinker or writer. He could not be concerned with the truth and be amusing at the same time. The word *serious*, thus, is supposed to mean no humor allowed. Chesterton, in a famous passage in *Heretics*, called "Mr. McCabe and the Divine Frivolity" (ch. 16), recalled being criticized. He said amusingly, using his words carefully: "The opposite of funny is not serious. The opposite of funny is simply not funny."[7]

Funny is not the opposite of serious. The opposite of funny is "not funny". What is true is not less true if it is expressed in an amusing way rather than in a stolid way. In fact, as Chesterton constantly demonstrated, wit enables us to see what is true more easily, more gently. No reason can be given why one cannot tell the truth in an amusing manner. In fact, often that is the best way to tell it. Even the very fact that some things are not funny is a sign of intelligence.

In the old comedy routine of Fibber McGee and Molly, McGee would tell a terrible joke. No one laughed except at the fact that no one laughed. His wife, Molly, in a famous phrase, would say: " 'T'aint funny, McGee." Then everyone would laugh again. Yet it is amusing when someone who muffs telling a joke is laughed at for muffing it. No one tries deliberately to tell "not funny" jokes. But we do tell jokes that are not, as it turns out, particularly funny for one reason or another. The telling of something we think funny often turns out to be not funny. This fact is itself rather amusing.

[7] G. K. Chesterton, *Heretics*, in *Collected Works*, vol. 1 (San Francisco: Ignatius Press, 1980), 159.

Few days would be bearable if we did not have laughter in them.

III

In what I call my "English book", as it was published in 1978, in England, with the odd title *The Praise of "Sons of Bitches": On the Worship of God by Fallen Men*, there is a chapter called "On Sadness and Laughter". So this is a topic that I have long considered. In that reflection, I had already come across the ironic fact that most famous comedians lived rather sad lives. Charles Schulz's comment at the beginning of this chapter rather confirms this observation. But isn't it a paradox to say that happiness is not the ground for humor, but sadness is? Joy comes about when we receive what is properly wanting to us—love, victory, reward. Laughter most often comes about when, unexpectedly, we get not what we expect or want but something else. Charlie Brown expects a baseball team. He gets a theological seminary. We laugh because we understand the incongruity of it all.

A question that has long haunted my mind, one that came up in the aforementioned essay "On Sadness and Laughter", was this: Would you abolish sadness if you could? At first sight, we all would say: "Of course we would." But at bottom, this abolition is the utopian temptation, perhaps the most dangerous of all temptations. It wants no pain or sadness in this world, preferably sooner rather than later, but down the ages if we must wait.

Moreover, such a mind thinks that it is possible to achieve these painless goals by man's own efforts, that what man can offer to man is really all he wants. No doubt, much pain has been eliminated or relieved. It is not a bad thing as such to want less pain or less sadness in the world. But generally, we do not eliminate these things but just postpone them or endure them. Not so many people die young in most civilized countries anymore, but they still die of other diseases and ailments later on, ones that they would have avoided had they died younger.

This question of sadness is not unrelated to the *Peanuts* character who says, on the theological mound: "But pain is a part of life." Would a painless world be a bodiless world? And if so, would that be an improvement over the one we have? Is it not a good thing that, in this world, beings with bodies as our own exist in the world, those that are subject to suffering, sin, and death? To be sure, we could eliminate such things by getting rid of the being in which they occur. No man, no pain. But that is the question: Is it all right for us to be the kind of beings we are, beings capable of suffering these things?

Yet we are not and are not intended to be angels. They have their own being and world. We cannot speak of pain in the angels; they are pure spirits. We can speak of their sin, however. Presumably, fallen angels suffer what is often called "a pain of loss". That is, they, as also rational beings, are vividly aware that they missed out on something tremendous because of their sin, because of their choice. They do not know what it is precisely. They have themselves as the alternative.

That not-knowing too is their punishment. But they do always know that what they received in exchange—namely, the choosing of their own autonomy—is not what really satisfies them. In effect, they got only themselves and not that for which they were created. Such is the ultimate fate of all free and rational beings who misplace the location of the delight for which they are ultimately created, the delight that comes from seeing God face-to-face, as Saint Paul puts it (1 Cor 13:12).

But what the angels experience is a spiritual kind of pain. It may be much harsher than bodily pain, as it often is also among human beings. Bodily pain tells where something hurts. It is a road map of our bodies. It has a purpose. It points to what is wrong. Without pain, we could not live for long because we would not know that anything was wrong with us or where it hurt. Spiritual pain, by contrast, has to do with our sense of loss at not attaining what we are for. This not-attaining could not happen if we were not free, since our choice of it is essential to its reality. It follows that sadness, delight, and freedom are connected. In the kind of beings we are—human, fallen, and redeemed— the three are related. Would we abolish sadness at the price of losing our minds and our freedom? We would not.

Aristotle says that some pleasures have pains as their opposites but that other pleasures have no opposites. Seeing simply goes on, as does thinking, with their own pleasures. Moreover, we would want these things even if they were painful. We want our tooth to ache when something is defective in it. Such pain tells us to do something about it. Generally speaking, if pain occurs, it is a sign of something wrong. The virtue of courage even seeks to guide our pain so that it does not interfere with the highest end of life. Indeed, Christianity exists, in one sense, to reconcile pain and suffering to our transcendent end. It is not an accident, then, that the Cross is a central element in Christian life.

Comedy and tragedy are the two great forms of theater. Tragedy is more solemn; comedy is more frivolous and lightsome. It treats lesser characters and less exalted emotions than does tragedy. Yet the greatest of the Christian poems is not called *The Divine Tragedy* but *The Divine Comedy*. Given Christian theology, not a few critics have concluded that no such thing as a "Christian" tragedy can exist. At the end, we are either saved or damned. Just judgment follows. No room for ambiguity about our fate is left open.

When we come to the last act of a tragedy, however, we feel and are purged of emotions of fear and pity, as Aristotle said. Things are put back in place. We see the way things are; even the mighty suffer the consequences of their deeds. "If this could happen to the great," we think, "what about us ordinary people?" And the fate of ordinary people is what Christianity is also about. Christianity recognizes the nobility of something worthy of honor and a result of superior intelligence or virtue. But it is also concerned with the fate of everyone. This latter concern is not apart from our freedom and our deeds, how we choose to live our lives, what we think of the truth.

In this sense, it is interesting that Charles Schulz conceives Charlie Brown as "everyman" because in fact we are all mostly losers. Only a few big winners are found. In World Cups and basketball tournaments, only one team finally wins. It is a far more important human experience to know how to lose than to know how to win. Winning in fact may be fraught with more spiritual danger than losing. Yet without winners there can be no losers. All enter the race, but not all win. If we take the world's fastest man in the 100 meters and let him run by himself, no one will pay much attention. He has to run against others, most of whom lose.

So again, I have stated that happiness and joy are much more difficult to explain than sadness and evil. At the same time, I have said that sadness and suffering are more typical of human life. Augustine explains this situation that finds happiness and sadness related. "Our Lord's words ["Blessed are they who deserved to receive Christ in their homes"] teach us that though we labor among the many distractions of this world, we should have but one goal", Augustine writes. "For we are but travelers on a journey without as yet a fixed abode; we are on our way, not yet in our native land; we are in a state of longing, not yet of enjoyment. But let us continue on our way, and continue without sloth or respite, so that we may ultimately arrive at our destination."[8] That is a striking phrase: "We are in a state of longing, not yet of enjoyment." We do have moments of enjoyment. How could we not? But we must also deal with the sadnesses and evils that cross our lives.

Still, is laughter compatible with evil? Are our sins subject to laughter? I have long thought of this question. Christ tells us that more joy is found in heaven on the return of one sinner than in the ninety-nine just who need no repentance. This insight, of course, was not a license for the ninety-nine to go out and carouse so that they could repent. But it does reveal something of the depths of sin and evil. At sin's bottom, as Blessed John Paul II said, we always find the divine mercy, forgiveness that can put it in place. It takes time to come to terms with the idea that there actually is rejoicing at the repentance of the sinner, not just his own rejoicing but that of others. We are pleased that others are forgiven. If we are not, like the brother of the Prodigal Son, we too can be alienated from the Father.

I have often thought (and hoped) that, on their being finally repented, forgiven, and punished, our sins eventually become

---

[8] Saint Augustine, *Sermo 103*, 1, in the Liturgy of the Hours, Office of Readings, Feast of Saint Martha, July 29, Second Reading, 3:1560.

occasions of laughter over how awful we could be and how
delighted we are to be rid of them. We will look back and
shake our heads in disbelief that we could ever have done
what we in fact did or, having done it, that we repented of
it. The salutation of the confessor is usually something like:
"Go now in peace and joy." These words are said to the
repentant sinner about his own actions that he recognizes
were wrong.

Christianity does not think it can absolutely stop men
with free wills from sinning, though it does not, of course,
intend to encourage it. It exists to provide a hope that,
when we do sin, it is not the end. We can be forgiven. The
great sin of despair is constituted by the belief that no forgiveness is possible. It is not true, but it is comprehensible
how someone in grave sin or even greater pride might think
that no forgiveness is possible. And it is not possible unless
God has provided a way for this forgiveness to come about
for each of us.

IV

In the beginning, I cited a passage by an old man, actually
Belloc himself, in his *Four Men*, a favorite book of mine.
This remark took place during a walk in 1902, in the south-
ern English county of Sussex. This was Belloc's home county.
He knew that the only way to record and keep what he
knew and experienced was to write about it. It is poignant
how fleeting passing things are, including humor and our
lives themselves. How little attention we often give to the
passing moment, itself full of wonder! If we someday return
to a place we know today, it will not be the same place or

create the same mood in our souls, either of sadness or of laughter.

The things of our kind are escaping us even amid the enduring and permanent things. Our friends die. New people come into our lives. We know both the fleetingness and the permanence. We also know that the permanent things outlast our own lives. The permanent things have been known and written about almost from the beginning by men who have now passed on. They have left their records of what they knew and saw in this world during their days in it. This record presents us with richness without which we could not be ourselves or know ourselves fully. Without remembering what happened before, we cannot really live in our own "now".

Among the "rational pleasures" of our lives, no doubt, wit and humor rank high. As I have said, a certain redeeming quality is found in them. When we can finally laugh at the things, even the worst things, we can put them into perspective. Of course, we know of things that are so horrible that no one could ever laugh at them. If we do not know of the depths of human sin, we have not been paying attention and we are dangerous even to ourselves.

This recognition of evil too is part of the human record that cannot be gainsaid. It is a permanent thing that dire things among us have happened, and not just wars. Terrible things also happen in the lives of the rich and the poor, the powerful and the unknown. Human laughter and delight exist in the same world in which unspeakable horrors happen. This was, no doubt, something understood "from the beginning" (cf. Gen 1).

But as Augustine said, "we are in a state of longing, not yet of enjoyment." We do long for a world in which such things do not happen. But we do not long for a world in which the enjoyment we now experience ceases. Indeed, we think that the laughter and delight are closer to the permanent thing from which we arise. We live lives in which we find sadness and delight, sin and goodness, tears and laughter. When we try by ourselves to separate them out, we find that sometimes the only way we can deal with evil is, as Socrates said, to suffer it. Surely this is the Christian lesson too. And what is striking about our wit, laughter, and delight is how suddenly and unexpectedly it comes upon us, almost as if we live in a world in which some kind of immense joy hovers about us.

Johnson said that it is not natural for a highwayman to take the road without his pistols, nor for a wit to appear without merriment. But if the merriment is always at the expense of God or decency, it is less than reasonable. The pleasures of such humor are jaded. We should not be surprised that almost anything good can be used in a harmful way. A good part of the adventure of life consists in using all things well and finding their proper pleasures. But using them badly, even humor, is also possible to us. From this latter possibility, much too can be learned. Sin is a moral evil that, nonetheless, is replete with intelligence if we would but see it.

"Happiness does not create humor." "Sadness creates humor." And yet the humor in our sadness points to what it is to be happy. We are given lives in which it is possible to err about the most profound things as well as the most trivial ones. This is the risk of being that, almost more than anything else, reveals the reasoning of the divinity: the fact that both the highwayman with his pistols and the wit who blasphemes God are present in our world. They are not the only ones, of course, but their presence suggests the sadness of those who use their talents wrongly as well as the plight of those who have to suffer from them.

Since in some real sense we are all sinners, however, we hesitate to recommend a world without vice, for that would leave most of us out of it. Ultimately, a world with no imperfect beings would be a world without us as we know ourselves. The risk of God, His humor, if you will, is that He lets the human drama occur. It carries itself to its own consequences. The attraction of the Good, however, remains. We see it in our best laughter, even finally in our sins. I would not want a world without sin if it meant a world without laughter.

But, of course, as I said, laughter precedes the Fall. The "reasonable pleasures" of mankind are not to be confused with the divine life, but they do not stand against it either. The divine life is divine. It is not lessened by the delight that creatures take in the proper activities of their own kind. And yet, in conclusion, we have the "longing". We know that we are not in a state of "enjoyment", because we understand that the laughter that we are granted is reflective of the abundance of joy in which we are created.

CHAPTER 3

ON PLAY AND SPORTS

Do you not see how people throw away their wealth on theatrical performances, boxing contests, mimes and fights between men and wild beasts, which are sickening to see, and all that for the sake of fleeting honor and popular applause?

—Saint Basil the Great[1]

Sir Joshua [Reynolds] also observed that the real character of a man was found out by his amusements,—Johnson added, "Yes, Sir; no man is a hypocrite in his pleasures."

—Boswell's Life of Johnson[2]

Exercise self-discipline, for you are God's athlete; the prize is immortality and eternal life, as you know full well....
... The good athlete must take punishment in order to win.

—Saint Ignatius of Antioch[3]

---

[1] Saint Basil the Great, Hom. De caritate 3.6, in the Liturgy of the Hours, Office of Readings, Seventeenth Week in Ordinary Time, Tuesday, Second Reading, 3:551–52.

[2] James Boswell, Boswell's Life of Johnson (London: Oxford University Press, 1931), June 15, 1784, 2:567.

[3] Saint Ignatius of Antioch to Saint Polycarp, in the Liturgy of the Hours, Office of Readings, Seventeenth Week in Ordinary Time, Friday, Second Reading, 3:564.

I

The passage from dogma to wit and humor, and thence to sports and play, is not particularly great. Laughter exists in this world. It too, as we have just seen, is an aspect of thinking clearly and correctly. Samuel Johnson agrees with Sir Joshua Reynolds that the real character of a man is revealed in his voluntary amusements. Character comes forth in how he plays the game. In American sports lore, we come across the oft-cited statement of the journalist Grantland Rice: "It matters not whether you win or lose but how you play the game." I have always thought the opposite is truer. If it does not matter whether you win or lose, no game is possible. The whole point of playing the game is to find out who wins and who loses, something worthwhile doing "for its own sake". This "finding out" can come about only by playing the game.

No one can play a game, be it tennis or basketball, with someone who is only out for exercise, who does not give a rap about winning or losing. Sports reflect life in this sense. We have to "want to win" to be what we are. In part, that is why sports are so instructive, much more than we often give them credit for. If we do not care how we live or how we play the game, we will be more than losers. Even losers play the game. We cannot live even tolerably well if we do not choose to live well, if we do not choose to enter the real game of life that wants to know how we played, how we chose, when we had a chance.

Good luck and accidents are part of any life or game. This is why sides or goals are chosen by the flip of a coin. But the playing itself implies discipline, strategy, alacrity, and stamina. The sports world reflects the real world in ways that

constantly surprise us. Almost the only place today where
we can find honest discussions of cheating, rules, excessive
vanity, real humility, and good and bad manners or deeds is
in the daily sports page. Here standards of excellence and
examples of perversity constantly come up. More often than
anywhere else, they are called for what they are.

As I have pointed out with regard to Charlie Brown in
the previous chapter, most of us are in fact losers in much
of what we do. We are good in one or two things but lousy
and lousier in most of the other areas. The few "best" always
imply the many that are not the best. But this is all right.
Revelation seems in fact to have been designed with losers
in mind, with the great many ordinary and not just the few
most excellent. This is why revelation is filled with words
like *salvation*, *repentance*, and *forgiveness*. Without the former,
the losers, we cannot have the latter, the winners. Be it so.

How to lose is one of the great lessons of life. Most of us
are not very old before we have a chance to learn it. I
remember losing a couple of boxing matches in high school.
It was, in retrospect, good for me. (No, I did not win any.)
Moreover, it is quite possible to lose poorly. It is never easy
to accept losing; that losing is difficult is in itself a good
thing. But there is something worse than losing according
to the rules of the game, and that is winning by breaking
them. We used to have a cry as kids: "Cheaters always choke!"
They don't, of course, but everyone knows that they should.
But if we have a game in which no possibility of cheating
exists, that would mean that it is a game not played by free
human beings, the only kind there are.

With many other moralists, Saint Basil the Great, however, bemoaned the great wealth spent on sports. I believe
the gross income of the National Football League in 2011–
2012 was 9.5 billion dollars, 60 percent of which went to

the players. Basil knew about games that were not so edifying, men fighting beasts or even men fighting men unto death, the infamous gladiatorial combats. Boxing we can see every day on television, with new rules in which we fight not just with fists and gloves but with feet and elbows. Wrestling in colleges and in the Olympics remains a serious sport, but on television it is mainly a gory entertainment. The professional quarterback Michael Vick got into considerable trouble by promoting dogfights. Basil did not like theatrical performances, but we presume that he was not referring to Sophocles but to the sort of things we now call "adult entertainment".

We must remember too how much sports mean to ordinary people. Polo may be the sport of kings, but soccer and basketball are the sports of the masses. They are diversions, to be sure, but they are not only that. We may spend too much for a ticket to see the Yankees or the Forty-Niners, but what we see is often a riveting event. If it is a good game, we are fascinated by it. Many great incidents happen in terribly played games. We are there to see the game, but what we see penetrates to the core of our being. We see unfold before us the game, the play of the athletes, the rules, the winning and the losing. We do not know what will happen until it happens. The fascination is there, in the game, in the event.

In this chapter, I wish to elaborate a thesis that has long intrigued me. It is one that I think is of interest in the lives of most men and women. I have written a number of essays and two small books on sports and games over the years.[4] The relation of sports and philosophy is something

<hr>

[4] James V. Schall, *Play On! From Games to Celebrations* (Philadelphia: Fortress Press, 1971); *Far Too Easily Pleased: A Theology of Play, Contemplation,*

not unexpectedly found in Aristotle, the "master of all who know", as Dante called him. Aristotle suggested that watching games was rather like contemplation. I spelled this position out in an essay entitled "The Seriousness of Sports".

After having read this essay, numerous students over the years have told me that they finally had had explained to them something that they always felt, that sports were not just frivolous pastimes. But no one had ever explained why. Games contain something that cannot be written off as merely seeking "honor and popular applause", as Saint Basil would have it. No doubt, some of this seeking is also present, but the honor and applause of the game contain profound insights into our nature and even into the nature of the divine. Booing at a bad game and cheering at a good one, moreover, strike me as proper responses to a performance, to a game, that is well or ill played. Etiquette applies here too, in proper proportion. This is why we see penalties for what is called "excessive celebrations".

It is estimated that over a third of the entire world's population, at one time or another, perhaps more, watch the soccer matches in the every-fourth-year World Cup. If they can afford it, people travel halfway around the world to see such matches, especially if their favorite home team is involved. Most of us stay home and watch the match on television or read of it in the papers. The fascination remains pretty much the same for rich and poor. To deprive the poor of their games on grounds of their not being elevated enough strikes me as a gigantic failure in understanding either games or the poor.

and Festivity (Los Angeles: Benziger-Macmillan, 1976); "The Seriousness of Sports", in *Another Sort of Learning* (San Francisco: Ignatius Press, 1988), 218–29; "Sports and Philosophy", *The Mind That Is Catholic* (Washington, D.C.: Catholic University of America Press, 2008), 251–60.

Much money, no doubt, is spent in promoting, putting on, and attending such events, both professional and amateur. The same relative interest and cost could be estimated of the Super Bowl, the NCAA basketball finals, the British Open in golf, the Stanley Cup in hockey, the Wimbledon Championships in tennis, and the World Series in baseball, as well in the Olympics during every fourth year. And this emphasis on championship games does not overlook the more local interest of ordinary athletic games in local clubs, schools, colleges, towns, and cities, things that are duly reported in most newspapers and online in the world and local media.

If we took all the money spent on the World Series or Wimbledon and gave it to the poor, many of the same poor would like to use it to watch the series. It is inhuman to think that the poor need only bread. The argument is not over whether they need it but how it is best provided to them, surely not by such redistributionist theses. Beyond this is the classic question from Scripture over whether man lives by bread alone. He does not. He is also, as Huizinga once said, *homo ludens*, as well as *homo faber* and *homo contemplativus*.[5]

This interest in playing and watching games, I think, is not a bad or harmful thing. Quite the opposite; on examination, this interest reveals something important about the human lot. Indeed, since such interest in sports is so widespread throughout the human race when men are free to enjoy them, I think that it reveals something of the divinity itself. Plato took this view also, and that is good enough

[5] Johan Huizinga, *Homo Ludens: A Study of the Play Element in Culture* (Boston: Beacon, 1950); also Hugo Rahner, *Men at Play* (New York: Herder, 1965); Robert Neale, *In Praise of Play* (New York: Harper, 1969); and Michael Novak, *The Joy of Sports* (New York: Basic Books, 1976).

for me. Thus, I like to approach this topic through Plato and Aristotle. They are still the philosophers who best reveal to us what the natural condition of man is about at its best (and indeed at its worst). The pleasures of the game, I say, are "reasonable pleasures". They manifest something basic in our nature.

Saint Ignatius of Antioch recalled the preparation, the training that must go into games. Getting into shape is hard work, as anyone knows who has tried it. Workouts and gyms are not just modern inventions. We have to prepare in order that we might experience the delight of the game, in which often a chance for pain and injury is connected with the very playing. Saint Paul said much the same thing in 1 Corinthians 9:24–25. In order to play well, we have to be ready to do so. No athletic season begins before the players have had time to get themselves into condition, to practice, to simulate real games that count. Surely, this lesson can be universalized. It was, no doubt, why Saint Ignatius of Loyola called his famous little book precisely *Spiritual Exercises*.

The things that are most worthwhile in our lives require similar preparation and understanding of what we are doing, whether it be playing tennis or acting justly. Once we are in condition, the things that initially seemed difficult become easy and second nature to us. We suddenly enjoy the benefits of prior training by forgetting about it and turn our attention to the game. We realize that we cannot bypass the preparation, the training, and the discipline.

We may not want to play basketball or lacrosse, of course. But we can never opt out of the game of life and the proper preparation for it. We still have to play it even if we do not prepare for it. One of the great temptations of human nature is that of sentimentality, the thinking that we can have what we want without going through the steps in which it is achieved, the steps that include knowing the rules of the game and the standards of human living. We all might wish to be on a winning team, but we cannot be there without the preparation and the talent that it takes. Sports or athletics, by their very nature, I think, teach us this lesson in the most direct way, one that few really deny.

II

Yet, in this chapter, I am not really arguing that sports are important because of what it takes to participate in them—the courage, the discipline, the skill, or the fairness. I do not underestimate this active side of sports. But a more passive side of sports can teach us something deeply profound about reality. Let us suppose we go to a good baseball game some pleasant afternoon. A total of 47,253 paying spectators show up for the game, say—the Giants vs. the Cubs. I was at such a game once, in San Francisco. I found myself somehow sitting in the high centerfield bleachers near some unexpectedly loud Cubs fans, who were roundly but good-naturedly yelled back at during the whole game by the predominantly Giants crowd.

We look down at the field of play properly set in order before us. We see the grass, the infield sand, the fences, the lines, the bases, the mound, home plate, the safety nets, the out-of-play rods. The fans are all there getting into the game. We hear the bat hit the ball. We hear the cheers or the groans of the fans.

On the field are eighteen men, four referees, the managers, the substitute players, and the bat boys. Altogether, some fifty men are involved in the game, not to mention the announcers, the people who sell beer and hot dogs, the groundkeepers, and the cops. But the eyes are mainly on the eighteen players, and of course, the umpires. This difference between 47,253 watching and some twenty on the field seems oddly disproportionate. You cannot get 47,253 onto the field. But the fans are not there to play the game, except in their memories of past glories or in their imagination. The fans are there to watch the game. A great number of people—47,253, to be exact—pay to watch something, a baseball game. Are they silly? Are they escaping from reality? Are they corrupting the culture? How does what they are doing make sense, as surely it must if we be rational beings?

No spectator at the game goes home after the game to claim that he should have been out there playing. Rather, he goes home to recount what he saw—the game, how it turned out, why. In a sense, the fan got what he paid for, namely, the game, how it unfolded, who won, who lost, who was the hero, who muffed it. Let us suppose, however, that, on the field, we saw the same number of players and officials, but no one was in the stands. Would it be the same?

No doubt, many a good game or match of tennis or golf has been played at which no one but the players were present, though, in this case, reflexively, the players become their own spectators. I would not dispute the fact that fans make a difference. Nor is there anything wrong with it. In a sport like handball or swimming, it may happen every day on some court or pool. But the fact is, good games or matches, be they cricket, volleyball, track, or hockey, draw spectators to watch them. Something is there that calls for spectators. They want to be there just to see it happen. We find an excitement in the game as we see it unfold before us. We are glad to be there. Why is this?

Most countries and individuals, no doubt, have their favorite game or team or player. The Australians have their own brand of football, as do the Canadians and the Irish (other than the "fighting" kind in South Bend). American basketball rules are slightly different from those of the Olympic game, but the difference has to be learned. Cricket is pretty much limited to the old British Empire, but those who watch it in India or Pakistan are rabid fans. The Chinese excel in table tennis, the Swiss in skiing, the Californians in beach volleyball. But all over the world, we find large stadia for soccer, tennis, basketball, football, track, hockey, lacrosse, and other such competitive sports.

These stadia are not always filled. Frequently enough, we see a stadium built for ninety thousand fans with only ten thousand sparsely seated spectators at a given game. It might still be a good game. We also find national championships with arenas filled to capacity and tickets being scalped that turn out to be very dull or lopsided games, devoid of much drama. Most people like to see underdogs win once in a while. Indeed, those who make their livings betting on games like to see underdogs win, given the right odds. Actually, betting games, games of chance, must also be included in these considerations. Professional poker has its attraction because it has its own drama.[6]

Another remarkable aspect of sports, besides the game itself, the players, and the spectators, is the reporting of games. Most city papers have their sports sections in the daily paper, often in the best part of the paper. Most

[6] See Roger Caillois, *Men at Play and Games* (New York: Free Press, 1961).

television stations report sports, some nothing else. Remarkably good writing is often found on sports pages, largely, I think, because we can talk freely there about right and wrong, good and evil, fame and ignominy.

We go to a game. We see it. But we also go home and read about it the next day, not just to relive it, but to see how others saw it, how it stacks up to other games in other places and other eras. Were the stars of fifty years ago as good as the stars of today? We will always find people who could not care less about sports, who think them frivolous or useless, even degrading or corrupting, as they can be if their spirit and rules are not present. But on the whole, something very healthy is going on here. Behind this fascination with games is a deep insight into human nature and its destiny. It is not that games are the most important things in the world, but, in their own way, I think that they prefigure what is. Our ultimate meaning can be brought to our attention in many ways, but one way, as I see it, is through sports when we carefully consider what we do when we see a good game.

What, then, do I make of all this interest in sports, in the playing, watching, and reporting of games? It reveals something important about what it is to be a human being. Up to this point, I have studiously avoided saying something like "Sports are a waste of time." The reason for this verbal avoidance is that in fact, that is precisely what I think they are. But the phrase "waste of time" has its own history and nuance. The phrase comes up most graphically in Antoine de Saint-Exupéry's famous story *The Little Prince*. Here the phrase takes on a new meaning that is central to what I want to say about sports and our ultimate meaning.

Speaking of flowers and, by extension, of friends, the Little Prince teaches us that we really do not love anything (or anyone) unless we are willing to "waste" our time with it (or him). In this sense, we might even define prayer as the time we "waste" with God. Actually, that is a pretty good definition of prayer. We have all experienced occasions when we would like to spend time with someone. But the other person is anxious to get on, to be about some other business. He has no time to "waste" with us. He is "busy". Spending time with someone does not mean that we have to be "doing" something, in the sense of something useful or profitable. We can, to be sure, spend time with friends by playing games with them. That is, we just want to be there, together. We are beyond the "doing" sort of activities that need to be done whether we like it or not.

No doubt, we eventually need to get back to work, to the daily chores of life, but the phrase "to waste one's time with someone" captures exactly that point of profoundest importance when we realize that we just want to be in someone's presence. Everything we do is designed that we might have such moments, or discover them if we do not know what they are.

Language here seems odd. "To waste time" usually has a pejorative meaning. We are doing nothing when we should be doing something. "Don't just stand there, *do* something!" We are treading water, we are doing everything else but what we should be doing. But in my present context, it means rather something more like "not wanting to be anywhere else but here". This is already where we want to be, the end of our desiring, as it were, not the means to get there. Some of this "not wanting to be anywhere else" is also found in being at a game and beholding it.

III

Let me now turn to the matter most at hand. In a book entitled *Reasonable Pleasures*, why should we talk about watching sporting matches of whatever kind? The reason is simply that watching a good game is in fact pleasing. I assume, of course, that we have actually enjoyed and been absorbed in a good game at least once in our lives. We have watched its being played out before us. We did not know ahead of time how it would turn out. We wanted to be there because it promised to be a good match. If someone does not have this experience, nothing further can be said. We can deal only with what we experience. But this beholding a good game is a fundamental human experience.

As I mentioned earlier, I have been struck by the number of students over the years who have told me that they had this experience of being fascinated by games but thought that it must be wrong to consider it important. The experience itself, however, is a fundamental one, such that if we have not had it in some form or another, we will be hindered in understanding the more profound meaning of our lives. Some experiences teach us about other experiences, almost as if that is what they were intended to do. Sports do this if we think about them. We must be careful, no doubt, to distinguish and to separate this thing from that—sports are what they are, not something else—but we should not deny that there is something important going on when we all have similar experiences in beholding a game unfold before us.

Aristotle, unfortunately, did not leave any extended tractate on sports as he did on ethics, poetry, politics, and so many other things. However, he did make some pertinent remarks that enable us to think more deeply about this common but curious topic. Aristotle said, for instance, that games are for their own sake.[7] That expression, something being "for its own sake", is of great importance. I use it frequently. It refers to an end and not to a means. We do something "for its own sake", not for the sake of doing something else, though we in fact do many useful things for the sake of doing something else.

Some things really are good. We do not want them to be anything else but *what they are*. We prepare and exercise to play the game; these are means to our end. But we play it for its own sake. It is the activity of the end, when we are where we want to be, and no place else. Aristotle further said that sports or watching games is, in this sense, like contemplation. Contemplation of the highest things, evidently, is more important than sports but also is something for its own sake. The analogy between sports and contemplation is revealing. We are to think about it.

But why would the great Aristotle compare watching games to contemplation, to the knowledge of the truth for itself, for no other reason than just the knowing of it? Music is like this also. We listen to it for its own sake, to hear much more than we expected. After listening to the choir and orchestra of the Accademia Nazionale di Santa Cecilia play music of Haydn, Beethoven, and Arvo Pärt in the Vatican, Benedict XVI reflected: "With this music the human genius vies with nature in creativity, gives life to various, multiform harmonies where the human voice also participates in this language, which as it were mirrors the great cosmic symphony." [8]

[7] See James V. Schall, "On the Seriousness of Sports", *Another Sort of Learning* (San Francisco: Ignatius Press, 1988), 218–19.

[8] Benedict XVI, "Address at End of Concert", *L'Osservatore Romano*, English ed., October 6, 2010.

In this sense, at a concert, or as spectators at a game, or at a theater, the audience stands in a similar relation to the reason why they are there. They are there for the music, the game, or the play. They are there to watch something unfold before their eyes or to listen to something proceed through to its end. They are absorbed into the action not as actors but as spectators, hearers. But they are spectators, who see what is happening. They can relate it to their own experience or to powers in their souls that they have not yet been aware of. They realize that this game, play, or concert that they behold or listen to is something from beyond their own inner self. Until they saw or heard it, they did not know of it. They suspect they have not exhausted the depths of such beholding or hearing even when they have finished watching. Games too "mirror the great cosmic symphony". Plato would be pleased.

But Aristotle also observes that those who watch a game for its own sake deal with something less serious than those who contemplate the truth. Behind Aristotle's remark lies the famous, almost mystical, passage in Plato's *Laws* in which he said that only one thing is really serious, and that is God. In this sense, all else is precisely unimportant. But this "unimportance" is by comparison with what is truly important. It means that other things for their own sake—and there are these—exist out of the abundance of things, however we explain reality's fecundity.

Things that need not be nonetheless *are*. Aristotle thus recognized that more than one thing exists that fascinates us. This is the great thesis, so much developed by Aquinas, that there really are things other than God. And we know them. In the light of Islamic occasionalism (i.e., in all reality only Allah acts, not things) and Western voluntarism (i.e., all is will, so it can always be otherwise, not *what it is*), this reality of things that are not God may be the most important practical issue of our time.

In our immediate future, what most needs defending is likely to be not God but that what is not God is real, not an illusion of our minds or God's. The highest things do not teach us, however, that the more ordinary things are completely unimportant or uninteresting. Quite the opposite. But the fascination of many existing things does not deny the possibility of something itself intrinsically fascinating to which we would turn if we could. This was Plato's point also.

Games belong to the class of things that need not exist but do. As such they have their own charm and reality. It is what Tolkien meant by "sub-creation".[9] We have it in our power to write novels about human beings who never existed in situations that never happened, yet we create something plausible, something that is true to life. Likewise, the games we play are held together by rules and descriptions of the action of the games. The playing produces a scene, an ongoing action with its own structure and progress.

What I am arguing here is that these games that need not exist, that are not the most serious things in existence, nevertheless have their own charm and fascination. They do something extraordinary. They capture our attention. They take us out of ourselves. Games have their own time in which their action occurs along with their own space that includes the spectators. The point is not that we have to attend every game that was ever played but that all games do have their own fascination, their own inner action that is worth seeing.

[9] J. R. R. Tolkien, "On Fairy Stories", in *The Tolkien Reader* (New York: Ballantine, 1966), 3–73.

We can put it another way. A good game again takes us out of ourselves. We may not think, at first, that we want to be out of ourselves. I mean here that we concentrate on what is out there, the game. But it is only when we are most "out of ourselves" that we are most ourselves. Things not ourselves become ours by our attention, knowing, seeing, and hearing. This "being concerned with others" out there playing is, in part, what it means to be a social being. We do not create the world. It is already there for us to behold, to encounter, to act in, yes, to use. We are beings with minds that enable us to know what is not ourselves. Indeed, unless we know something other than ourselves, we cannot know ourselves. We are not the first object of our minds. Anything else but ourselves is.

Not only do we speak of our minds taking us out of ourselves, but we find that our loves do the same thing. While it may be true that we are also to love ourselves—"Love thy neighbor as thyself"—the fact is that the primary object of our loves is not ourselves. How terrible it would be if it were! The main object of our lives is the object of our affections, the who- or the what-is-out-there drawing us to him or it. Both mind and will imply this intrinsic "other" orientation of our being. The ancient saying went *Ubi oculus, ibi amor*—Where thy eye is, there is thy love. That is almost a perfect expression of this point. I bring these facts up in regard to games because of the experience of good games taking us out of ourselves.

We are, of course, aware that it is we ourselves who watch the game unfold. But our attention is not on ourselves. We suddenly find that we do not think of ourselves but of what we behold before us. This experience eventually takes us to the divinity, as we shall see. The experience is something totally absorbing. Yet it is we who behold. It is remarkable that we have intimations of this experience every day in things like games or concerts or theater that in fact find us living a life outside of ourselves. The experience of even one thing for its own sake is what best prepares for the final gift that is not ourselves but that for which we exist. The essence of human existence is that we are gifts, even to ourselves, but we do not give ourselves to ourselves. This is why, as Chesterton said, it is gratitude more than anything else that defines our reaction to *all that is*.

The analogy between watching a game and beholding the highest thing, the Godhead itself, may at first sight seem improbable. But Aristotle's awareness of the experience of things for their own sake is a keen insight into what must constitute this experience of the highest things. The closest that ordinary people come to understanding what is meant by contemplation comes from this experience of being outside of themselves in following a game. We even lose track of real time and put ourselves in the time of the game.

To the extent that we do not become so absorbed in it, the game does not fully arrest our attention. But to the extent that good games fully arrest our attention, to that extent, on reflection, we can glimpse what we call the vision of God, our end, the Beatific Vision that takes us outside of ourselves into the very Trinitarian depths of the Godhead while allowing us to remain the human persons that we are.

We deal here with yet another "reasonable pleasure". As I shall remark in the following chapter, many of the most important things about us are not those we accomplish ourselves but those that are given to us from the abundance of things. However, we do actively receive those things that are given to us. Even watching a game is an active thing, as we are alive to its ongoing accomplishment.

We are beings who receive even our own existence. But, having received it, we are present in the world full of things already made, as well as of things we make and participate in. It matters whether we win or lose, as it matters how we play the game. But these things that exist "for their own sakes", our games, need not exist, nor do we. We belong to that category of things that are important by being unimportant, by not being themselves the compete explanation of *all that is*.

CHAPTER 4

ON BEINGS TO WHOM THINGS HAPPEN

The ruins of the cathedral of Elgin afforded us another proof of the waste of reformation. There is enough yet remaining to show that it was once magnificent. Its whole plot is easily traced.

—Samuel Johnson, *Journey to the Western Islands of Scotland*[1]

What have you that you did not receive? If then you received it, why do you boast as if it were not a gift?

—1 Corinthians 4:7

[*Sally to Charlie Brown:*] It's that same girl on the phone again.... She says she's an old friend of yours. [*Charlie listens with perplexity.*] She insists on coming over to see you. She says she hasn't seen you for a long time.... [*Charlie wonders who she is. Sally concludes:*] I warned her that she'll probably be disappointed.

—Charles Schulz, *Peanuts*[2]

---

[1] Samuel Johnson, *Journey to the Western Islands of Scotland*, ed. A. Wendt (1775; Boston: Houghton, Mifflin, 1965), August 26, 1773, 17.
[2] Charles Schulz, *Being a Dog Is a Full-Time Job: A Peanuts Collection* (Kansas City: Andrews and McMeel, 1994), 103.

I

In the previous two chapters, I recalled, from the example of Charlie Brown, the fact that lives are often poignantly populated by what are called "losers". Games must have losers if they be true games. In the great college basketball tournament each year in March, of sixty-eight teams, sixty-seven go home losers. Someone beats all but one of them. The law of entropy seems to hold that in the end, everything will have spent all its initial energy. All will become inert. The very universe is destined to be a loser.

The antientropic principle, however, holds that, within the universe, a power exists that can originate something new. The human mind is the primary antientropic power in the universe because it can understand what is not itself and the relations of things in this cosmos to each other. It is not simply matter. And yet the human mind, extraordinary as it is, does not cause itself to be or to be mind or to be located in a body that it needs to begin to know. It does not initially think, "Let us make ourselves a mind", and then issue a fiat, Let it be! It already is a mind when it begins to think. It is already active as mind before it asks what mind is and whence is its origin.

Human history is naturally filled with accounts of what human beings do, with their deeds, both for good and for ill. One might say that history is a record—or better, a memory—of what has happened primarily under human agency. Of course, some happenings that have nothing to do with human causation are also elements in human history—floods, earthquakes, tornadoes, volcanic eruptions, crashes, and falling meteorites. But we remember even these largely because of the way people met or ran away from them.

Other human things are also themselves events outside of the control of the persons who suffer them. The person who is murdered or robbed does not plan to be murdered or robbed; otherwise, it would be a suicide or a giveaway. From the viewpoint of the children, divorce is usually one of these things that "happen" to them. One could say that most of the casualties of any war are also of those who had something "happen" to them outside their own agency. One might say the same for people in periods of economic depressions, as well as in periods of prosperity.

What interests me in this chapter are the things that "happen", and not just to us (but those too). I admit that most often the focus of our attention is on what we or others do. More real drama exists among us human beings because of our freedom than anywhere else in the physical cosmos. We look for reasons and motives of human actions. We want to find the human causes of things that might have been otherwise. And even in the case of natural disasters, like the 2005 New Orleans hurricane or the 2011 Thailand floods, many look to what human agents should or should not have done, to what they should have been prepared for but were not. We look for someone to "blame" even for natural disasters. Something curious is at work here.

In almost any natural disaster, we are not happy until we find some human agency to blame or praise for the disaster's occurrence or its alleviation. Whom, after all, do we blame for a hurricane or an earthquake or a volcanic eruption? Surely we cannot accuse the hurricane itself! It is doing what it is supposed to do. If we blame God, we must also praise Him for the water of the ocean and the winds of the seas. Other eras spoke of such disasters as "acts of God". They simply meant that no human agency was involved. These events just happened, though not without a hint of providential purpose.

What human beings did as a result of such disasters is, no doubt, of great significance. It reveals much about the character of a people. Did they do nothing? Did they expect others to do everything for them? Did they help themselves? But some excess of human pride is suspected when we seek a human cause for everything. We are reluctant to see that we are not the only actors in the world, that we too are rather finite.

A doctrinal or first principle is found here also. Nothing gives what it does not have. If something new occurs, this something new must first be there to cause its presence to be noticed. We human beings are the lowest of the intelligent beings in the universe. We are intimately connected with matter in all we do. But we are not only matter. Everything in us is ordered to our knowing, and acting through our knowing.

Yet many things just "happen". Theologians have argued that even chance events have intelligibility in the mind and providence of God. There is much truth here. Perhaps it explains why we always think that something is not fully explained by saying that it is merely a matter of chance. It is possible that chance and providence, without ceasing to be what they are, are not necessarily contradictory.

Of all the peculiar things about our existence, a most obvious one, but one too seldom reflected upon, is the fact that we are simply here. Things happen to us because of it. We are beings to whom things happen. They just do. We can do little about it. On reflection, we see that this fact that things happen to us is essential to the kind of beings we are.

We read in Scripture that the rain falls on the just and on the unjust. Scripture also indicates that natural events

can be instruments in God's purposes. This divine aspect
would not necessarily render chance events any less fortu-
itous in their own order. Indeed, those philosophic or theological theories that rid themselves of chance, such as Muslim
occasionalism or scientific determinism, end by undermin-
ing any proper human activity. Everything is reduced to
necessity with no element of freedom in it.

II

Here I wish to call attention to this more passive side of
our being. We pay too little attention to it. In one sense,
the most obvious thing about us is that neither *what we are*
nor our existence is of our own making. We begin in receptivity, or, as I think more profoundly, we begin in gift. We
are usually more attentive to those things that we cause to
happen or that others have caused to happen to us. The
fact that things can and do happen to us is itself a profound
insight into the limited kind of beings we are. But it is all
right that we be the kind of beings we are. Nothing pejorative can be found in the mere fact that we are not angels
or gods. All being, as such, is good, including our own.

Nothing happens to God outside His own being except
what He allows to happen. God already has what is worth
happening. But I would again stress that it is all right to be
a limited being. It is all right not to be a nobler creature.
The alternative to our being limited beings is not to be
unlimited beings; rather, it is not to be anything at all. We
human beings do not have the choice of becoming gods.
But God had the choice of not causing us to come to be in
the first place. Thus, at the root of our being is not only

God who created us but the nothingness out of which we were called and given existence.

A flash flood occurred one summer weekend in a state park in Arkansas in 2010. Several families who had been camping there were lost in the raging waters. The water level rose so quickly upstream after downpours in the night that no one really expected such flooding. By all human standards, it was a tragedy for these normal families out on a weekend camping trip with the kids. Such things, of course, happen every day on larger or smaller scales someplace in the world. Indeed, their relative frequency makes most of them invisible to us, though today natural tragedies in almost any part of the world are for a time widely reported.

Sometimes chance events are happy, or so we think. We win the lottery or get an unexpected job. It rains just at the right time for the crops. Winter snows provide water throughout the year and good ski slopes in the winter. At other times, chance events are upsetting and sad, like the flash flood in Arkansas. But even with these chance events, we ask questions about providence and meaning.

Thornton Wilder's famous novel *The Bridge of San Luis Re* was concerned with precisely when the bridge over the high ravine accidentally broke. Each person who went to his death was at that precise moment when God most wanted to call him. Accidents seem to be part of or included in the order of things as if at some point they belong there *as* accidents. We can grasp the notion that an accidental death may not be accidental in the plan of God.

To conceive a world with no accidents is to imagine something out of our experience. Things of chance enliven and threaten our daily lives. Yet accidents reveal purpose, or better, cross-purpose. One thing going one way crosses another going another, neither intending to cross the other but doing so. Both are moving purposefully. In this sense, our meeting of almost any other human being involves an element of chance, but also something more than chance. Things occurring by chance are simply doing what they are intended to do. Rain falls. Rivers overflow with too much water for their normal capacity. People meet in out-of-the-way places.

The two Aristotelian categories of action and passion, that is, of acting and being acted upon, are related to each other. These categories already indicate the existence of things that need not exist but do. Moreover, we have the constant distinction between things that happen to us through "natural" causes, such as floods, and those that are caused by the intervention of willed human agency, such as the destruction of the cathedral in Elgin earlier mentioned by Johnson.

And, of course, we have the Charlie Brown dilemma. When we see someone "again", will we be disappointed? Indeed, if we see anything at all, even for the first time, will we be disappointed or, perhaps more often, delighted? An ex-student of mine told me of receiving two tickets to the opera *La bohème*. She invited a young gentleman friend to go along with her. When they came to the final curtain, she was weeping. But the young man said he saw nothing meaningful in the opera. He was totally unaffected by it. Strange as it seems, it is possible to be unmoved by the great events and beauties of our world. It happens all the time to many, if not most, of us. It is quite possible indeed not to be moved by the world itself, by the fact that it exists at all. The problem is not with the world but with us.

But, in principle, we cannot see anything at all unless it is already there to be seen. Our very seeing depends on what is already there. Neither our sight nor our intelligence makes the things we see and identify. They are unaccountably before us. This experience, that things really exist, is itself a wonder to us. There *are* things. We have a capacity to apprehend them even as they remain what they are, which, if we are wise, we want them to do. We give ourselves neither our capacity to know nor the things that are there to be known. Without their very passivity, their being there, we could not perceive anything.

What concerns me here is the notion of being acted upon. We normally think of a sick patient as someone who is operated on or acted upon. The patient's only task is to be there with the condition that needs attention. The medical analogy is obvious, but the category of "being acted upon" is broader than this common experience. The patient, with the primary aid of his own body and the help of doctors, is to be restored to what he was or ought to be. A patient is already a something. Soil itself, for instance, is acted upon when we plant oats in it or when rain falls on it. The planting and rain happen to it, though it is itself already a certain kind of thing capable of receiving seeds and rain. The seeds of oats do not grow to be watermelons.

Here I am concerned not so much with resistance to being acted upon but with the fact that we are the beings to whom things happen from various agencies originating from outside of ourselves. Without these agencies, of course, we could not live at all, even though human living is not essentially "being acted upon", though this latter is essential to it. Our existence presupposes and requires myriads of things like sun and wind that act on us whether we like it or not. In this sense, it is quite all right to be a dependent being. The alternative to such dependency in our case is not being at all. We keep coming back to this possibility of our not being at all as fundamental to our understanding the kind of beings we are.

III

Such reflections already bring up the question: Is anything found that is *not* acted upon? That is, complete dependence implies by contrast pure activity somewhere. That the world is full only of things acted upon is impossible. Activity stems from the kind of being the thing is. Each thing acts according to *what it is*. Horses act in the way of horses. Planets act in the way of planets.

Each thing has an inner natural order by which, in its activity, we recognize it to be this thing and not that. It is a dog, not a lion. In our experience, most things must first be acted upon before anything else can happen. However, unless those things are there already, nothing we can do follows. We cannot act upon what is not there. The greater mystery, proposed over the ages by many different philosophers, is this: Why is there something, not nothing? The question is crucial, for from nothing we can only get, well, nothing.

Socrates is famous for his observation "It is better to suffer evil than to do it." That is, he suggests that having evil things done to us is better than our doing wrong things to others. This is a counterintuitive position. It distinguishes between doing things and letting things happen to us. This Socratic phrase touches on a deep mystery—namely, the relation of passion to action, of things acting and being acted upon. Christians who know of Christ's suffering have to pay attention to this reality of being acted upon. Whether we do evil or suffer it, both are factors in our actions. Obviously, to suffer it rather than do it is what is good. If we cause others to suffer because of what we do to them, we cannot then escape some judgment on our own activities. We were the cause; he suffered because of it.

Some things that we do ought not to be done. Not every action is good, even if it is possible to do it, which obviously it is or the issue would not come up. Thus, "suffering" evil implies the power to recognize what the evil is that we suffer, or else there would be no sense in suffering it. There would be nothing noble about suffering for the sake of suffering itself, as if to say—as Buddhism sometimes seems to say—that existence itself is a suffering. When we say it is "better" to suffer evil than to do it, we imply that suffering, being acted upon, is not itself a neutral thing. Indeed, it may be salvific, as the examples of both Socrates and Christ teach us. It is not just that we are acted upon but that it is better for us to be acted upon by someone else than for us to do the same evil action. This understanding is already implied in the very notion of a patient. A patient is acted upon because an outside agent deals with him.

"Being acted upon" is a phrase well worth much reflection. We are beings with the capacity of looking out on the world from a vantage point within us. We each have our own unique existence. We, ourselves, are aware that we are not at all the initial cause of our own existing. For us, being acted upon is a primary experience. The nature of human infancy is a long period of being acted upon by others if we are to live and flourish. Our existence bears the mark of having been put there, not of our having put ourselves there. Philosophers tell us that the two most basic questions we can ask of our situation are: (1) Why is there something rather than nothing? (2) Why is this thing not that thing? Things are, but they are in different ways. We exist in a human way that is not itself a product of our own making.

To the first question, one might wonder whether "nothing" is not the most passive of things. Is nothing the ultimate patient on which something happens? But this approach is to think of nothing as if it were something. Nothing passes from nothing to something. Theologians are careful to say that the phrase that God created "out of nothing" does not mean that nothing is some sort of material that God found floating around to form into the world. Nothing happens to nothing. This principle is why actuality stands before any thought about nothing. We cannot and do not begin in nothing, though we can by negating something catch a glimpse into what "nothing" means. The quality of being acted upon presupposes something there to be acted upon. We have to begin with the fact.

In this sense, passion—being acted upon—presupposes that something is there already. And many different kinds of things are already there. One thing is not another thing. So the beings to which things happen are already what they are. What I find fascinating about the notion of a being to which something happens is the fact that a world is revealed to us that seems to want our attention called to it. If something happens to me, something that I have no control over, it shows the degree to which I am not in total command of my life or being.

But it also shows me what sort of being I am, though perhaps I never noticed. Do I really want to be a being that is totally in control of everything? If so, would I still be the kind of being I am? Would that be good? And is not that the real issue, whether it is all right to be the kind of being I am? This reflection teaches us that something apart from God or nothingness in fact exists, though not necessarily by its own self-causality.

We can relate the fact that things happen to us to another more graphic idea, namely, that things are gifts to us. We sometimes, of course, speak of rain or wind or sunshine as gifts. What else could they be? It does not seem sufficient to call them mere necessities. This way of speaking is itself somewhat curious. If things merely happen to us, nothing more needs to be said, though we do note that we need other things to be the kind of beings we are.

The notion of gift adds something more. It suggests that the things that happen to us have a source that is not just determined to act the way it does. We can conceive the whole order of passivity as itself a gift. In this sense, things are unexpected, but they do not come about for no reason at all. It is not uncommon in, say, Christmas gifts, that we get as a present what we need and want. Yet something that comes to us as a gift has a different status from what we purchase because we need it. Moreover, many gifts are as such useless. If a lady is given a dozen roses, she cannot eat them. The gift implies a relationship beyond need between the one who gives and the one who receives.

What seems essential to the notion of gift is that something comes to us, something happens to us, not merely by chance, though we did not anticipate it. A gift is also something that comes to us from the outside. From our point of view, gifts also just happen to us. In receiving gifts, we are like medical patients. We are there and we are acted upon. The patient is properly acted upon only if the action from the outside be directed to his own good. That is the difference between good and bad medicine. This fact that things are directed to our good does not deny that the accidents that can happen to us from the outside can also be destructive. We are the kind of beings to whom good and bad things happen, sometimes caused by nature, sometimes caused by free agents.

Earlier, I mentioned that I am not concerned here so much with resistance to things happening to us. Obviously, we need to protect ourselves. We build shelters against sun and rain. We seek to prevent free agents from abusing their power over us. In part, we organize ourselves into societies in order that we might protect ourselves and provide for what we need. We limit the ways things can unexpectedly happen to us. We know what can happen to us. We know what kind of beings we are. And yet, would we want to be in such total control of things that nothing could happen to us except at our sufferance? We would, in that case, conceive ourselves after the manner of a divine being, of only action and not passion. In that case, we would cease to be what we are.

We are the beings to whom things happen. We suffer what comes along to us. We also learn what kind of beings we are from suffering such things that happen to us. When things happen to us, we are usually aware that they do. What happens to us enters our soul. This is the kind of being that we are. We are the kind of being who receives existence, who receives much of what he needs from the agency of others. But is it all right that I am the kind of being to whom things happen?

Should I not be in revolt against my very being and its condition? Should I not refuse to accept the precept "It is better to suffer evil than to do it"? At a most profound level, we can say that the highest human nobility is not found in doing but in suffering. But the suffering is what upholds what is good. Suffering is not for its own sake. Only if this is so, that suffering upholds the good, can we be given what we are.

This understanding of suffering is counterintuitive, of course. We are not beings split in two, one part passive and one part active. In a sense, all of our being is both active and passive. When things happen to us, we know them. We know what they do. We provide for what we need, knowing what happens to us when we do not. We thus should not be disappointed in the kind of mortal beings we are, beings to whom things happen. This capacity is what initially opens the world to us, both as a world that is simply there and a world that is given to us, as if there is an order, a reason, in the giving, in the being able to receive.

At one end of this consideration of the things that happen to us is the suffering of evil rather than doing it. Given a choice between suffering evil and doing it, suffering evil is nobler, as it upholds what is good. But is there a place for receiving even if there is no question of evil? The other end of considering things we receive is covered by gifts. The essence of a gift is that it is not a repayment in justice. If I return something I borrow from another, I am not giving him a gift. Gifts do not belong to the order of justice. The reduction of everything to justice means the elimination of gifts. If everyone has a right to everything, we can give them nothing. For if anyone lacks something, the reason is that someone else has deprived him of it. Hence, if he later receives what he thinks is due, it deserves no thanks since it was already in principle his.

The receiving of gifts, then, is the highest form of receptivity. A gift is not due to us. It is given out of abundance and not as a payback. Our relation to God is conceived primarily in terms of gift, not justice. God is, of course, just and calls everyone to judgment. His gifts are beyond justice. The essential dogma is that God need not have created anything but Himself. God did not owe anyone creation or existence. But He could give us existence. And once existence was given, He could also call us to an end that is higher than any purpose that might be inherent in our human nature. Thus, both our existence and our being called to eternal life are gifts.

Once the gift of life and supernatural life—that is, the Trinitarian life to which we are personally called—is given, however, God is not free to rescind its terms. If we are created free in such a fashion that we must choose to love God and our neighbor and, in addition, actually carry out this choice, God must be faithful to His word. In heaven, we find no rational creatures who do not choose to be there. Otherwise, if He automatically saved everyone no matter what his thought or deed, He would be acting, and we would not.

And this is the drama of our existence; namely, how do we live given the gifts of life and salvation? We can be given the highest things and still reject them. This brings us to the next chapter, on hell, on the final rejection of gifts. Hell, of course, is presumably not a pleasure. But, I think, its consideration does yield to us a "reasonable pleasure". When we see its logic, we see that God is not responsible for our final choices.

CHAPTER 5

THE "REASONABLE" CASE FOR HELL

Those who are deemed incurable because of the enormity of their crimes, having committed many great sacrileges or wicked and unlawful murders and other such wrongs— their fitting fate is to be hurled into Tartarus never to emerge from it.

— Plato, *Phaedo* [1]

Minos the dreadful
Snarls at the gate. He examines each one's sin,
Judging and disposing as he curls his tail:
That is, when an ill-begotten soul comes down.
It comes before him, and confesses all,
Minos, great connoisseur of sin, discerns
For every spirit its proper place in Hell.

— Dante, *Inferno* [2]

I think almost all the crimes which Christians have perpetrated against each other arise from this, that religion is confused with politics. For, above all other spheres of human

---

[1] Plato, *Phaedo*, in *Plato, Complete Works*, ed. John M. Cooper (Indianapolis: Hackett, 1997), 113e.

[2] Dante, *Inferno*, trans. Robert Pinsky (New York: Farrar, Strauss, and Giroux, 1997), ch. 5, vv. 8–11.

life, the Devil claims politics for his own, as almost the cit-
adel of his power.

—C. S. Lewis[3]

I

Hell is a place into which no one, presumably, wants to
plunge or descend. But everyone is pleased to talk about
it. Everyone has an opinion about it, if only to reassure
himself that it does not really matter or apply to him. The
common view about hell today is that, really, it does not
exist, or if it does, no one has to worry about it. Even if
it exists, no one goes there. No everlasting fires have been
sighted. We cannot take it seriously. It need not factor into
any of our calculations about how we live. God is too
kind to send anyone there. He will, in any case, figure out
how to save any fool who managed, by his own fault, to
arrive at its famous gates. Not even the Devil or the worst
of criminals, not to mention the ordinary lot, need to give
up hope.[4]

Besides, on an empirical level, no astronaut has located
hell, though some mightily hot places in the cosmos have
been observed and measured. *Hell* is also a rather popular
cuss word. "Go to hell!" is an oft-heard directive that we
address, usually in desperation, to people who cross us.

---

[3] C. S. Lewis to his father, August 10, 1953, in *The Collected Letters of C. S. Lewis*, ed. Walter Hooper (San Francisco: Harper, 2007), 3:358.

[4] See James V. Schall, "The Natural Restoration of the Angels in the Depths of Evil", in *Faith, Scholarship, and Culture in the 21st Century*, ed. Alice Ramos and Marie George (Washington, D.C.: American Maritain Society / Catholic University of America Press, 2002), 251–68.

Hell also can be used to emphasize the greatness of something. George Bernard Shaw wrote of Sean O'Casey's 1928 manuscript of *The Silver Tassie*, "It's a hell of a play."[5]

Just as in the Old Testament, the word for heaven became a substitute for naming God, so *hell* is a catchall word symbolizing the fate of all who reject the Good in some final affirmation. Plato called it Tartarus. The Bible calls it Gehenna. We can use whatever word we want; the essential idea is that a "place" exists in which all the injustices will be requited. Plato arrived at this position before the Christian era and independently of the Jews. Its existence is also a postulate of the human mind thinking on itself, especially, with Plato, on the ultimate requirements of justice.

Howard Kainz, referring to a book by Ayaan Hirsi Ali, an atheist and a former member of Parliament in the Netherlands, wrote:

> The fear of hell partly drives the cruel and almost sadistic subjugation of women in Islam, many of whom are locked into marriages in competition with other wives and prevented from any normal exposure to the outside world. Ayaan's mother, grandmother, and most other women in her clan, according to her account, were willing to live like slaves or worse, influenced largely by the numerous graphic and almost obscene descriptions in the Koran and other sacred books of the tortures of hell reserved for those who do not accept or who depart from Islamic tenets.[6]

---

[5] Eileen O'Casey, *Cheerio, Titan: The Friendship between George Bernard Shaw and Eileen and Sean O'Casey* (New York: Scribner's, 1989).

[6] Howard Kainz, "Cautious Reflections on Hell", *The Catholic Thing*, August 29, 2010, http://www.thecatholicthing.org/columns/2010/cautious-reflections-on-hell.html. The book Kainz refers to is Ali's *Nomad*.

Thus, the fear of hell is so great that it justifies everything from subjugation of women to terrorism against innocent infidels.

This contrast between the no-hell faction and the fear-of-hell-justifies-all faction shows us that hell is a delicate topic. If not adequately understood, it falsifies the reality we face. However, as I will argue here, hell has something very positive about it. Thinking clearly about it even gives us a certain, yes, "reasonable pleasure". Without taking it seriously, we are likely to trivialize our ordinary existence, which we should be at pains to defend. The denial of any truth, including that of hell, usually leads to a grimmer world. Each of the teachings of revelation, including hell, has this about it: when we try to deny the teaching, we end up somehow also compromising the integrity of our minds and their relation to things.

Over the years, I have given a good deal of thought to the importance and meaning of hell.[7] Indeed, I am rather fond of the topic, but not in any morbid way. Insofar as Western culture at least refuses to consider the main point of the doctrine of hell, just to that degree is the doctrine more worthy of considerable attention. Hell proves to be a surprisingly fertile intellectual reflection in its own right. If we think things out, as we are intended to do, often they make more sense than we, at first sight, are wont to grant. Hell is one of these topics that shed much light on human existence as well as on the divine reality. Some think that

[7] See James V. Schall, "On the Neglect of Hell in Political Theory", in *The Politics of Heaven and Hell: Christian Themes from Classical, Medieval and Modern Political Philosophy* (Lanham, Md.: University Press of America, 1984), 82–106; "Regarding the Inattentiveness of Hell in Political Philosophy", in *At the Limits of Political Philosophy* (Washington, D.C.: Catholic University of America Press, 1996), 89–102; "The Brighter Side of Hell", in *The Modern Age* (South Bend, Ind.: St. Augustine's Press, 2011), 73–84.

the teaching on hell was revealed to us to make us fear punishment. I tend to think it was first given to us to make us think, and to be careful where we tread.

The chief resident of hell, of course, is the figure known, among other less prominent names, as Satan or the Devil. It is often remarked that, in efforts to present the Devil in literature or on stage, he ends up stealing the show. He becomes a rather amusing and shrewd character who, after all, is not all that bad. He is clever, witty, and charming. But not for nothing is Satan is called the "father of lies", after his telling Eve that she would not die if she ate the forbidden fruit. Hell and lies have a strange affinity that cannot be passed over lightly. It goes back to the Word that is truth. God does not lie to us, but the Devil does.

First of all, we must establish some argument to show that discussing hell in the modern world is not a frivolous or worthless pursuit. For a while, after World War II, when we realized the great crimes of Hitler, Stalin, and Mao, it was difficult to think of a suitable punishment for their deeds other than hell. The subject comes up again in considering the millions of innocent children killed in abortion mills by presumably rational beings. It is difficult to admit that there is simply no ultimate punishment for these unforgiven and unacknowledged crimes against the innocent of our kind.

Hell is something revealed to us in Scripture, though, as Plato shows, a reasonable basis for it is found in the notion of unpunished violations of justice. The idea is found in other religions in various forms. I cited Plato at the beginning of this chapter. Many of the things that Christians understand about hell were already present in Plato. Indeed, the best way to approach hell in the modern world is through Plato. This way of understanding why this doctrine might make sense, might be "reasonable", has the advantage among

the Gentiles of not being associated with Christian revelation as such. Hell is something that seems quite reasonable
and logical once its terms are spelled out. Christian revelation merely reaffirms and clarifies it. Catholicism takes its
reasonable basis for granted.

II

In Plato, the issue of hell arises out of the inability of politics to accomplish its own task, that of establishing justice
in community. C. S. Lewis was quite perceptive to locate
the main power of the Devil among us midst the politi-
cians, among whom lying and injustices are not unknown.
Why this association of hell and politics should be so is
worth some consideration.

Generally speaking, we have three understandings of the
nature and origin of government among men. The first is
the Augustinian notion that government is a result of the
Fall. Without the Fall, we would have had no need of coer-
cive government. But, in all societies, in all ages, men reveal
a constant presence of crime and injustice. These crimes
and injustices must be faced. Government is presented both
as a remedy for this disorder and often as a cause of it.
Rulers, however designated, are not immune from such moral
disorders. We cannot expect it to be otherwise in this life.
Our end lies elsewhere. All we can do even with the aid of
good government is seek to minimize and reduce the levels
of disorder within each polity.

The second understanding of government is that of Aristotle. Man is by nature a social and political animal. He has
a common good that requires him to establish an order of

rule among the various people and interests that are found in actual polities. The purpose of the polity is the natural end of man as a mortal. It is to bring forth the various potencies that are found among men. These potencies are to be placed in an order of good use where they can support and reinforce one another. Aristotle was not unaware of the corrupt side of human nature. Still, he thought that political rule was good and necessary to bring forth the best in human mortal existence and to prevent the worst from having free reign in the civil order.

The third understanding of government or form of rule, almost modern in its scope, is that found in the Apocalypse. Here, with the Roman Empire at its worst in mind, we have an absolute form of rule in which politics absorbs all of man's life. It becomes itself "a mortal god", to use Hobbes' term. In this sense, politics can present itself as an alternative to God. It can propose to be itself the source of morality, the distinction between right and wrong.

This same notion was found in Christ's temptation in the desert, where the Devil, in effect, posing as the ruler in C. S. Lewis' sense, offers Christ the rule of the nations if, falling down, He but adore the Devil. One could make the case that this absolutist or totalitarian form of rule has become more, not less, prevalent as time has progressed. The real battles are between those nations that think politics is a limited rule and those that place all power in their rulers' hands.

The Platonic background, however, is most instructive. The polity was set up in order that injustices be punished and that those to whom honor was due would receive it. It turns out that, in human history, it has never happened that, within one polity or era, all crimes have been requited or all good deeds rewarded. Not even close. This disturbing fact means that as one age dies and another takes its place, we have generations and eras of violations of justice that have never been justly resolved by human political authority. The questions then arise: Must this abiding injustice be the case? Will all actual human political regimes end in the same situation?

Plato's "city in speech" was described as the one regime in which justice was fulfilled in every case. In other words, it seemed possible to describe such a regime, but it was not possible to establish one. Every effort in human history to establish a perfect regime, and there have been many such efforts, has usually ended in producing something worse than normal regimes with their mixture of good and bad. The best we could do in practice was to produce less dangerous regimes and hopefully more virtuous people. The effort to improve on this situation by human means usually ended in making things worse. The logic of Plato's position was, then, that the world seemed to be created in injustice. This conclusion appeared to be a fact of our common experience. At the origin of things, then, in this view, was not the Good but injustice.

Plato, of course, was not satisfied with this conclusion, logical as it may have appeared. Discussion of heaven and hell thus comes out of classical political philosophy over the revulsion of granting that the world was made in injustice, even though this conclusion seemed evident from the record of actual men. Plato's answer to this puzzling situation began with his surprising affirmation that the soul of man was immortal.

While in prison, on his last day with his young friends, Socrates argued that the soul of man was indeed immortal. The immortality of the soul, in this sense, is a postulate of political philosophy, or better, the truth of the immortality of the soul is confirmed by something that arises in political philosophy and experience, namely, the status of justice in the world. The issue is not: How does a good God allow hell? but rather: What happens to those who commit terrible crimes but are not punished?

Plato treats of the judgment that follows individual human lives in four places: once in the *Republic*, once in the *Phaedo*, once in the *Statesman*, and once in the *Gorgias*. The point of the myths, however, is the same. All seek to establish the same point, namely, that in death we shall all be judged for our deeds. Immortality is simply a statement that assures us that we will be there for the judging.

This judgment is, even in Plato, a consequence of our relation to the Good or to God. That is, our sins are consequent on rejecting a basic principle of reason or of what is right as manifested in our lives no matter when or where we lived. This lack of reason or order is why every sin, in some basic sense, is a repetition of the sin of pride. Or to put it in Old Testament terms, it is a repetition of the Fall of Adam and Eve. We elevate our own judgment to be superior to that which is found in reason.

Thus, hell is not something that God set out to create as a show of His great power. He did not first create it and then look around for someone like you or me to put in it. Hell is always a consequence of something of vast importance that went before and without which we could not be, that is to say, the fact and use of our free will. But the result of judgment is never determined; it always presupposes free will and responsibility. The logic of judgment presupposes other realities, that is, free will.

The temporal sequence may not be the same as the logical sequence. That is, we may confront the fact of punishment before we understand the reasons for it. Hell is always a consequence that flows naturally and logically from other principles. I do not want to say that hell is merely a "logical" idea. Still, the logic of the need for punishment indicates that its reality makes sense and is not simply irrational.

In Plato, as in the Gospels, a Last Judgment is described for us. Benedict XVI in his encyclical *Spe Salvi* has reaffirmed the basic centrality of this teaching. At the same time, Benedict sketches out what happens when the reality of a final judgment is rejected as unimportant or when it is assumed to be nonexistent. Basically, it reappears in other, more dubious forms. If the human soul is not immortal—that is, if nothing passes beyond this life—it follows that injustice and justice have the same results. Great crimes of injustice are gotten away with and great examples of courage or generosity are unrewarded. If either of these results is the case, then the world is made in injustice. It is rationally incoherent. It was this frightening alternative that Plato fought against, as we do also. In our imagination, we may concoct a world in which the reality of judgment and hell has no place. But we must say of our imaginative hell-less world that it is not the world in which we actually live.

In *Spe Salvi*, Benedict brings up the case of two Marxist philosophers, Theodor Adorno and Max Horkheimer. Working off of the same justice premises we found in Plato, these philosophers see that we must postulate not only the immortality of the soul but also the resurrection of the body. We must do this if it is ever going to be possible that those who actually committed the greatest of crimes but went unpunished, or were punished insufficiently, are to be given their due, that is, to receive justice. What Benedict is driving at, of course, is the fact that both the doctrine of the immortality of the soul and the more precise one of the resurrection of the body are necessary if we are frankly to confront the Platonic question of whether the world is in fact created in injustice.

In many discussions of hell, the point of view is this: How could a good God punish someone eternally? But coming from the Platonic background, the issue is rather posed like this: If such crimes are not punished properly, the world is incoherent. In other words, it would be even crueler if our anguished minds knew that the greatest crimes were not punished or the greatest deeds not rewarded. The further question arises whether those crimes that were punished by the courts or whether those noble deeds that were rewarded by the state (or by anybody else) were adequately or properly requited. This approach puts a new light on the issue of God's relation to hell, particularly to its essence. The essence of hell consists essentially in a choice of oneself over any other good. Hell is not a "God problem". It is a human problem because of man's freedom.

The reason the Marxist philosopher unexpectedly posited the necessity of the resurrection of the body, and not just the immortality of the soul, as Plato did, was because, though he did not believe it, he understood its logic. That is, he recognized that the only way justice could actually come about would be if the actual person in his completeness, the one who committed the crime, were confronted with it. What troubled the Marxist philosopher was this very same problem of justice that bothered Plato.

We can talk all we want of God, but here we are talking of the experience of men in this world, actual men whose deeds are accurately described. We are talking about the actual human record. What we see is that if no hell exists as a possibility for punishing actual human beings who commit grave crimes and sins with no thought of repentance, then we must give up on any notion of ultimate justice. This same conclusion was basically Plato's position.

III

We might grant such logic but still insist: Why would a good God ever put us in a position wherein this possible hell was open to us? The answer is, briefly, that God had no other choice if He was going to create free beings capable of loving Him in the first place. If He chose not to create anything, which He was free to do, the issue of hell would never have come up. For it is quite clear that had there been no creation of cosmos, angels, or men, there would be no hell. But would this be an improvement?

Hell has nothing directly to do with God. It is an unintended, but necessary, consequence of creation itself. Hell does have something to do with what God was seeking to do in creation. Remember, hell arises out of realistic considerations of justice. God is also just—each is rendered his due. Justice questions concern beings that are free to be just or unjust. Hell has to do with the record of injustice that in fact exists in the world of rational and free agents in their relation to God and each other.

Saint Paul indicated to the Romans that the sufferings of nonrational beings were in fact related to the status of the rational beings (Rom 8:19–23). Essentially, God was not trying to create a free being that would justly go to hell. Rather, He created a free being that was capable of loving himself, other beings like himself, and God. Such a free being was capable also of rejecting such love, divine or human, because he was created to be free. Without this power of rejection, neither love nor damnation would be possible or conceivable.

Within this consideration, the issue of hell comes up. If any created, finite being, including man, was really free, it would be necessary that this being could reject the purpose for which he was created, ultimately God Himself. He could reject this purpose even if the purpose constituted objectively his own happiness. His rejection, however, would be posed in terms of a good. If he could make this rejection, then we have "invented" hell. Basically, hell, together with the immortality of the soul and the resurrection of the body, allows the free creature to live forever with his choice or definition of what is his good or purpose in being. Hell is the living with the consequences of his choice. Hell is not God's purpose for him. God wishes every man to be saved, as Saint Paul said (1 Tim 2:4).

God will, of course, do everything that He can to call man to his created and transcendent purpose. But He cannot make the being, once He created it, not to be what it is, that is, free. Even God could not make something free but then change His mind about it once He saw what man would do with this freedom. The creation of man included allowing him to be free. The point is clearer from the other side; that is, if the free creature does choose God, to love Him, that too has to be a free choice. God wants everyone who loves Him to choose freely to do so.

This freedom to choose oneself over God is the opposite side of love, which allows us to choose what God has created us for, namely, to live His own internal Trinitarian life. God thus, as I like to say, took a risk in creating such a free being. He risked that such a being might choose not to love Him even with the being and gifts that He gave to him. Once God created such a being, He had to let it act in its own way. The story of this acting is what we know as history and salvation history. God does not just create us and leave us alone. At every instant, we find some additional direction or guidance to remind us of our highest destiny, but even this grace, as it is generally called, can be rejected. Otherwise, God alone would be acting, not us.

We catch some of the flavor of this approach when we recall Christ's chastisement of the small towns around His own birthplace. He said that in the judgment it would be better to be in Sodom and Gomorrah than in Bethsaida or Chorazin (Mt 11:20–24). Surely something similar could be said of every small town in human history. If it is possible to save our souls in even such obscure places, it is also possible to lose them there. This is but another way of saying that Christianity is a universal teaching that includes everyone in whatever time or place he may live.

Chesterton reported his grandfather as saying that he would be grateful for existence even if he landed in hell. That was a striking phrase, but it touches a paradoxical truth. Presumably, a person in hell is still grateful for his existence as a human or an angelic being. He does not want to cease to be, to be annihilated as if he did not ever exist. Moreover, he would know that his situation in hell is not due to God or to his existence itself but to his own choice. He would have no one to blame but himself. This "no alternative" realization is, no doubt, the most agonizing punishment of hell. It means the spending of eternity with only one's choice to keep one company. The person in hell concomitantly realizes that he still would not make another choice against what he has already chosen.

IV

The title of this chapter is "The 'Reasonable' Case for Hell". With some amusement, some wit might have called my arguments rather "A Hell of a 'Reasonable' Case". This phrase could go either way, meaning either a terrible case or a great case. One last line of argument about hell, however, can be spelled out. Let me approach the issue this way. Years ago, I recall once reading a remark by the then well-known New York philosopher Sidney Hook. He observed that there are certain things that we would prefer not to know about a man.

What would these things be that we would not like to know? If a man betrayed his country or his friend, or his wife, for instance, we would just as soon not know this about him. We may have to know it if we are involved or if we are an official dealing with the case. But we would just as soon not know, unless, of course, we had to fear that the man might do it again. At the same time, we do need to know that the possibility of betraying country, friends, wife, truth, and good is quite possible. Such betrayals happen all too often among our kind.

We are, moreover, considering hell in a book called *Rational Pleasures*. If we wish to know someone else, we best know something of his character—his virtues, his vices, his habits, and his tendencies. We might ask again: What is the significance of each individual, unique human life? Each human person has an ultimate purpose to know and love God and his neighbor. It follows that our own destiny is bound up with what we hold and how we treat others. The commandments to love God and neighbor are contained in one whole that sees the neighbor as also created by God for God's own purpose, not ours, though God's purpose is, in fact, our real good.

The doctrine of hell is important and sensible at this point. Dostoyevsky's novel *Crime and Punishment* had to do with whether it was possible to kill a thoroughly insignificant and mean character without any compunction or danger of guilt or punishment. It turned out not to be possible. That conclusion brings me to the last point that I should like to make in my case for hell. I consider this point, its understanding, to be, as it were, a "rational pleasure". I say that without irony. The relation of hell to the objective dignity of each human person is close indeed. This position does not mean that we cannot sin or repent of our sinning. It includes both possibilities.

Indeed, the notion that Christ came into the world to save us from our sins is the other side of free will. It is the divine response, as it were, to creating free-willed beings in the first place, only to have some of them, at least, use their power to reject God's ways. God could not make the will not to be free. He could forgive the sinner, but only if he would be forgiven. Accepting forgiveness too involves freedom. This divine response to offer forgiveness is, technically, "beyond justice". But it does not deny it. It presupposes it. We ourselves can easily despair if we use our will badly. We cannot forgive ourselves. But we can be forgiven.

The Incarnation was a divine response to human sins. It took away neither the possibility of sinning, as we see in subsequent human history, nor its consequences. But it did give sinners another chance. And this other chance was that of restoring our wrongs by acknowledging that our own choices did not trump those of God as spelled out in the commandments. Repentance is nothing less than restoring to order what we chose to reject. We live with the consequences of our sins but, on repentance, no longer with their self-justifying principle, which is that of preferring our will to God's reason in giving us being.

The pleasure of hell? Hell, I think, is the one doctrine that most graphically grounds the importance of each individual person on a daily basis. Essentially, it means that, at any moment in my life, I can commit a crime or a sin that would justly have hell as a consequence if unrepented. And even if I repent, I still may need suffering when I see the consequences of my wrong spelled out in the damaged lives of others. This sense of the need to acknowledge the consequences of even our forgiven sins is, as Benedict said in *Spe Salvi*, the case for purgatory. We do not see or want to see God unless we have fully distanced ourselves from sin.

But a definite pleasure arises when we recognize the importance of each of our acts. That is, we realize that, at any moment, in any place, any human being can do something to someone, however insignificant, that is so heinous that it merits hell. Such is one of the very meanings of human dignity. This possibility indicates how important each person is in God's eyes. Hell is the classic doctrine that, in a kind of reverse logic, teaches us our ultimate importance. We do not establish the criteria of what is right or wrong; we discover it, hear it, and learn it. We do not cause right to be wrong or wrong to be right, even if we act and speak as if we can. When we act on our own standards, not God's, we create our own subjective world. But we still remain in God's world. What I call the "rational pleasure" of hell is simply its role in emphasizing to us the enormous significance of each human act of each existing human person.

Let us look at hell from yet another angle. Let us suppose that hell did not exist. That is, suppose no ultimate retribution for our unrepented crimes and sins is possible.

Would this ennoble us or degrade us? Logically, this no-hell possibility would loosen any bond that existed among human beings. If nothing we could do would merit hell, then it really does not make any difference what we do. Hell, in this sense, is the guarantee that human life is important. Free creatures can abuse both themselves and others by their free acts. While hell, in one sense, emphasizes the consequences of our acts, in another sense it is the guarantee of our acts' ultimate significance. We do not live vapid lives that make no difference. We live lives of such importance that we can deserve hell because we do not recognize our dignity and that of those with whom we dwell.

Hell's presence, in this latter sense, is felt every place where free will is found. In a graphic manner, hell makes every human life potentially of transcendent significance. No unimportant lives or instances in life can be found. This approach does not suggest, of course, that we have to live unsettled and cautious lives out of fear of hell. It does mean that we are aware of our dignity. We realize the consequences that come from violating it.

This approach explains why I think hell is a positive doctrine. It gives us grounds for a "reasonable pleasure". What appears, at first sight, to be a purely negative and frightening concept turns out to make considerable sense. Indeed, it brings order back into the world. The world is not, in fact, made in injustice. No one is punished unjustly. No one escapes the justice due to his free acts. All can be forgiven if they will. God would not have it otherwise. He could not make a free being not to be free. He could not permit a free being to escape the logic of his choosing himself over others.

The reasonable case for hell is quite direct. Its reality undergirds the importance of each human person in all of his actions. However much we may downgrade or ignore human worthiness in each person, we cannot escape the fact of each person's importance in the eyes of God. Something remarkable, even amusing, is found in the realization that hell is the other side of human dignity. But this dignity includes not just any definition of this dignity. That dignity also depends on our understanding of its truth and our actually willing the good in man that we did not ourselves create or formulate or put there. By teaching us the worst that can ultimately happen to us, the doctrine of hell underscores the abiding importance of the best in all of our human acts.

CHAPTER 6

THE EARTHLY CITY

But Dionysius [of Syracuse], seeing how we all felt, and apprehensive lest our fears might lead to something even graver, treated us all kindly, and me [Plato] especially he reassured, telling me to have no fear and earnestly begging me to remain; for there was no honor for him in my leaving, he said, but only in my remaining. For this reason he made a great pretense of begging me, but we know that the requests of tyrants are mingled with compulsion.

—Plato[1]

It is clear then what must be the quality of the citizens of God's City during their earthly pilgrimage.... They must live by God's standards, not man's.... In contrast, the city, that is, the society, of the ungodly consists of those who live by the standards not of God but of man.

—Augustine, *City of God*[2]

---

[1] Plato, Seventh Letter, in *Plato, Complete Works*, ed. John M. Cooper (Indianapolis: Hackett, 1997), 329d.

[2] Augustine, *City of God*, trans. Henry Bettenson (Harmondsworth, England: Penguin, 2003), 14.4–10.

When benevolent planning, armed with political or economic power, can become wicked is when it tramples on
people's rights for the sake of their [the people's] good.

—C. S. Lewis[3]

I

The phrase from Hebrews 13:14, "here we have no lasting
city", is a familiar, even a haunting, one. The second American president, John Adams, to recall our last chapter, once
remarked that hell is the most political of all the Christian
doctrines. Hell is, as it were, a lasting city. The indirect
result of this lastingness is that the actual, passing cities that
we know in our mortal lives do not have to claim divinity
for themselves. Not all justice questions have to be settled
by men in this world. To pretend to be able to do so, in
effect, is a divine claim by a human agent. Questions beyond
human capacities do not have to be solved by human enterprise, even when we consider them, as we should. Exact,
just, and final punishments can be left to God. This realization frees the earthly cities, with their often awesome
powers, from the temptation to be themselves gods.

Actual cities, though necessary, are prudential institutions in their configurations. They are less than perfect, finite,
a bit chaotic—human, in other words. This lastingness of
hell is indeed provocative. In principle, hell is lasting because
the human will that causes one's place in it does not choose
to change. Hell's lastingness is itself contingent on our choice.

[3] C. S. Lewis to Mary van Deusen, July 2, 1951, in *The Collected Letters of
C. S. Lewis*, ed. Walter Hooper (San Francisco: Harper, 2007), 3:92.

Hell does not cause hell to be hell. Free rejection of grace and good "causes" it. We remarked earlier that some "rational pleasure" is found in thinking about hell. That pleasure consists principally in seeing its inner logic. Hell is a consequence of one's own free choice. It would not exist if free choice did not exist or, better, if free choice were not used badly. It is not imposed arbitrarily from the outside by pitiless gods but grows logically from inside a human soul. It is the result of someone's making himself what he wants to be, not what God wants him to be.

What is the relation between the cities that last and those that pass away? No human city lasts. The only lasting cities are heaven and hell.[4] Human cities, however, are designed to last longer than individual human lives, the threescore years and ten. Human cities are filled with individual persons, imperfect each of them, who, in their plurality, are continually coming into and passing out of existence. Cities exist during the temporal mortality of human beings. The city is not itself a substance or a person, a thing that exists for its own sake, with its own "body" and separate existence. But it does depend on existing human beings for its relational reality outside of nothingness.

The polity, following Aristotle's categories, is a real relation of order or disorder of citizens to each other. "That the earthly and the heavenly city penetrate each other is a fact accessible to faith alone", the Vatican II document *Gaudium et Spes* stated. "It remains a mystery of human history, which sin will keep in great disarray until the splendor of God's sons is fully revealed." [5] The earthly and the heavenly city

---

[4] See James V. Schall, *The Politics of Heaven and Hell* (Lanham, Md.: University Press of America, 1984).

[5] Vatican Council II, *Gaudium et Spes*, 40, Holy See website, www.vatican.va.

"interpenetrate" each other. In other words, both realities are present in the same place, in the same lives.

Within actual cities, human beings decide the lasting city in which they will abide. This deeper activity of ultimate choice is what lies beneath the surface of the politics in all actual cities. Space and time allow the arena for this final decision to be made, with room for gradual development, relapse, and repentance. Such is the final, indirect purpose of the actual earthly city, in which, one way or another, everyone passes his mortal life. Without the civic arena of multiple actions that reveal the souls of men in their relation to one another, we could have no true test of the nature of our loves and our being. Without the real test, all else would be mere pantomime. The doctrine of hell, as we suggested previously, is, paradoxically, what indirectly guarantees the absolute importance of each existing human person while he is existing in the earthly city.

John Adams had the sober realization that no human government could punish all crimes, nor should it seek to do so. Both Plato and Aquinas understood this issue in the same way. If a government tries to right all wrongs or reward all good deeds—and not a few governments have tried—it becomes itself absolute. On its own authority, it imitates a divine power and an omniscience that it does not possess. Its laws and decrees claim to define good and evil with no further reference but to itself. Human government, however, is in principle limited in what it can reasonably know and provide. It can know only men's external acts, as Aquinas said, not men's inner human motivations. The knowing of internal motivations is again a divine prerogative. But government can know that things like theft, murder, fraud, and other violations of human dignity are wrong and need to be prevented or restricted.

Governments that do not acknowledge any transcendent purpose to individual human lives or the manner in which they should be lived do not see themselves limited to the external order. They can demand not only external but internal assent and obedience for the sake of unity. This is, in part, the heritage of Rousseau and his famous cultural project of absolute spiritual unity that requires the "free" assent of everyone, even if it has to be "forced". The great problem of human politics is the limitation of politics itself to a common good that has as its main purpose bringing out the goods that potentially exist in the polity's actual citizens. This is why C. S. Lewis, in the introductory citation, rightly warned that the most dangerous of earthly cities are those that manipulate human dignity in the name of what they themselves conceive to be and define as the human good, this independent of all natural or divine order.

II

Civil societies, however, rarely last more than two or three centuries while retaining the form of their initial founding. Even if names like China, India, Egypt, England, Greece, and Spain go back centuries and centuries, the forms of government within them have changed radically, often many times. Aristotle understood this fact. The United States, by this criterion, turns out to be one of the oldest political forms in the modern world, though this judgment presupposes that no radical changes have taken place in its form. Many think that the American government is no longer ruled by the principles and constitution of its founders.

What is the scope of the earthly city or, as it is called, man's political life? Aristotle remains the best guide. Basically, man is by nature a political animal. This affirmation means that the many capacities and talents found in individual human beings cannot be manifested or flourish if everyone has to do everything. If everyone has to do everything, no one can do much more than barely stay alive. But it is good and natural that wide varieties of things, institutions, and accomplishments be brought forth. This endeavor requires specialization, which in turn requires rules, interchange, subordination, and order. Men united in cities can do amazing things, as history teaches us.

That men need to form a political order is by nature. However, the particular structure that this order takes varies and is a product of prudence. Wide varieties of good, less good, and bad political structures exist at all times and in all places. But many good forms of rule and many bad ones can be identified. All men in fact live in more or less imperfect regimes, ones that could be better or worse. The various goods that man is capable of producing or developing, including those of the spirit, can come forth in relative harmony only within a polity. Politics basically deals with man during his mortal life as he pursues the variety of goods open to him. The spirit and structure of a polity may make it easier or more difficult to practice virtue, but ultimately this practice remains in the hands of the individual person.

All cities are composed of human persons who bear the substantial reality of being. The political society is not another "being" alongside human beings. It has no soul to save. Rather, the frontiers and borders of a state indicate the particular order whereby public life is lived within a given polity. The offices of rule—executive, judicial, and

legislative—can vary in number, configuration, and powers, but they will always be present. The state is not something to be imposed by some higher power onto the people
to guide or control them. Rather, it arises from the activities, controversies, and needs that occur among acting people. Disputes need to be settled. Laws need to be known
and evaluated. Responsibility needs to be located. Crimes
need to be identified, prevented, or punished. Goods and
services need to be produced. Meanwhile, the lives of the
citizens go on within the political arrangement in which
they find themselves.

Aristotle classified the different regimes of cities by their
ends and the location and number of the ruling authority.
He spoke of monarchy, aristocracy, and polity as good forms
of rule; tyranny, oligarchy, and democracy as disordered forms.
These regimes could be a mix of these forms, such that
one polity might possess all three good forms. He was concerned both that there be a reasonable principle of rule and
that the citizens continue to manifest their own virtues and
souls in their ordinary lives. Citizens were basically to be
responsible for themselves.

Aristotle in fact thought that most regimes were either
oligarchies or democracies, both bad regimes in his classification. They ruled either for the sake of wealth or of a
kind of unlimited or random freedom rather than for the
sake of a rule of virtue according to the classical understanding of the different virtues open to men for ruling
themselves. Indeed, the law was itself designed to help citizens to rule themselves. At its best, law commanded the
acts of the virtues. It was not merely a rule but a rule that
pointed to what was worthy of doing. Aristotle's classifica-
tions remain uncannily valid and useful even in modern
states that purport not to be based on virtue and look to

no natural human order of the good. Aristotle's democracy came close to anticipating them.

III

What is of interest in this chapter is not the particular configuration or classification of civil societies, but why we have civil societies in the first place. This endeavor to distinguish one polity from another on the basis of some criterion of human excellence or vice is, of course, a worthy one. Aristotle's distinction between best regimes, tolerable ones, and bad ones is valid. Human beings do have a purpose while they live in the earthly city. They should strive to build and live in better regimes in order that they might live better lives. Preventing a regime from getting worse is itself a worthy political project. One can still fail in a good regime, or succeed in a bad one. But this possibility is because of the fact that habit influences, but does not determine, how we live.

The great illusion of the twentieth century was that we could "force" men to be virtuous by careful planning of their politics and economics. No automatic path to virtue, however, exists in any regime—socialist, liberal, or whatever. Even disordered regimes maintain that they are good regimes for their people here and now. Evil, corruption, and disorder will be found in all actual regimes, not because of a defect in constitutional structure, but because free will is operative in each of the regimes' citizens. How citizens are dealt with defines the worthiness, or lack thereof, of the regime.

Yet, looked at in another way, one wonders whether the configuration of the regime one lives in makes much difference. As I like to put it, it is possible to lose one's soul in the best regime and gain it in the worst. More people may well have gone to heaven from concentration camps and gulags than from civil societies that live a more peaceful life but also manifest widespread individually corrupt existences. Such is no argument for concentration camps, of course, but it does remind us of what is at stake. *The greatest of political temptations, again, is to construct a system that supposedly guarantees each citizen both happiness and virtue simply because of his civic membership without any action of his own.* Generally, this rationale is the justification for socialism in most of its forms, the automatic making of men "good" by a system and not by virtue, self-discipline, and choice.

The transcendent activity of gaining or losing one's soul, however, goes on in every regime, whatever its external structure or theoretic rationale. "If you are wise, then," Saint Robert Cardinal Bellarmine wrote, "know that you have been created for the glory of God and your own eternal salvation. This is your goal; this is the center of your life." [6] We need also to examine regimes by the criterion, not of prosperity or physical well-being, but by that of living according to natural reason and the virtues. It is quite possible that the most prosperous regimes are the ones in which more wickedness is found, as opposed to poorer ones, though much can be found in them too. The culture of abortion, if no other, makes this possibility of much vice in wealthy societies quite clear. Aristotle accepted the fact that much evil was present and would

[6] Robert Bellarmine, *On the Ascent of the Mind to God*, in the Liturgy of the Hours, Office of Readings, Feast of Saint Robert Bellarmine, September 17, Second Reading, 4:1412.

remain in all polities. The Christian doctrine of original
sin adds an explanation to this presence and its persistence.
It does not offer any prospect of this-worldly perfection
through the manipulation of politics or economics.

Scripture talks of "end times" (Mt 24; Mk 12). At the
end of the human dispensation on this earth, we will still
find marrying and giving in marriage, plowing and planting. People will be going about their ordinary affairs, no
matter in what kind of actual regime they live in. Of course,
we do not need to postulate anything so striking as "end
times" to make the same point. Every day, men and women
pass out of human existence on this earth by accident, sick-
ness, old age, war, terrorism, or self-destruction. "We know
neither the day nor the hour" (cf. Mt 25:13) is a familiar
admonition of the fragility of our earthly existence. In any
case, the span of human lives, even if it is a bit longer in
areas with good medicine, always comes to an end. Earthly
cities remain, now populated by other individuals who have
come into citizenship by birth or immigration to replace
those who pass on.

What I should like to do here, then, is to relate the earthly
city, in which most human beings live or have lived, to the
transcendent city into which they come at death, the "lasting" city of either heaven or hell. Earthly cities have their
own glory. They are worthy institutions in which both noble
and heinous things happen. Men live and die in promoting
and defending them. Few states last more than several centuries without being destroyed or changed so radically as to
be unrecognizable from what went before.

Within the city, issues of good and evil are everywhere
present. They are manifested in the lives of the citizens.
The state, in its Augustinian concept, exists primarily to
mitigate the enormous power of evil that occurs in public

life through the actions of individual citizens within it. This idea is more complicated because the state apparatus itself may be the source of the greatest of the evils. "Who shall watch the watchdogs?" is a political saying of great moral insight. The rulers are themselves human beings subject to original sin. Psalm 118 reads: "It is better to take refuge in the LORD than to put confidence in princes" (v. 9). In the history of mankind, probably the greatest crimes against innocent human beings have been political crimes. Such crimes would include the deaths of both Socrates and Christ.

Scripture uses the analogies of kings and kingdoms to describe the city in which we shall finally settle. This analogy keeps the social nature of our existence, including our happiness, before us. Actual cities are in part the domain of justice. The first responsibility of a civil society is to provide for at least a minimum of just order. This responsibility will include the power of coercion, that is, courts, army, and police. At present in the world, we find perhaps two hundred political entities, most of which have within them subsidiary bodies that carry out various functions of justice and order.

Aristotle and Plato did not think that politics and economics were the same. The provision of material well-being was not the primary function of the polity, though everyone recognized that such things needed to be provided. Producing and distributing sufficient food, clothing, and shelter for a people on a massive scale is a modern invention. Generally, we know how to do this. If people have not a sufficiency in basic areas, it is most often due to political or ideological reasons or moral corruption, not to a lack of knowledge about how such goods are produced. Many refuse to learn or apply what is known to produce what is necessary. They prefer dishonest means. Arguments between free markets and socialism persist. The political order is usually a support for the economic order and should not itself become identified with it. The relationship between the two is mutual; both need each other.

Both the Old and New Testaments presume that "the poor" will always be with us. Yet the relative riches of others can make us feel poor even if we already have what we need. The requirements of neighbors are looked on both as individual responsibilities and as political ones. Indeed, one of the most obvious things that give glory within the city is its capacity to assist citizens in their basic needs. The proper way of any political order to provide for everyone is to enable people to help themselves. Looked at in this way, our aim is not to help someone else but to enable everyone to help himself in a fair exchange. But even when all of economic goods are provided, the essential task of the city only begins. The city exists that something higher than politics can go on within its confines.

IV

Political society has its own gravity. Its importance depends first on the dignity and the reality of the individual members who compose it. Its importance also depends on the worthiness of its members' human lives. Such virtuous living is not automatic but depends on the use of their free wills. Man is not for the state, but the state is for man. The state ought not to be an impediment to man's attaining his highest end, though it often is. The whole relation of state to church revolves about this issue. The first political question is thus: What is man for? The common good includes and enhances the good that already exists in him. He has a twofold end, that which can be attained in this life, a political happiness within mortal life in the city, and a transcendent end, the lasting cities. The two are directly related but not the same.

If man were the highest being, Aristotle said, politics would be the highest science. But man is not the highest being. Thus, politics itself, even with its own purpose, looks to a human end that is beyond politics. The things that are not political, things of truth, goodness, and beauty, are already beyond politics, as is human fate at the end of life. The political order enables these things to come forth in their own reality. Politics serves them; they do not serve politics except in the sense that polities depend on truth, goodness, and beauty to be what they are. This is why it is possible to say that earthly cities ought to be reflections of a city that is higher than themselves. The power to imitate God in a finite manner is indeed a human gift and accomplishment. Such a power is based on the fact of our own intellects and wills proper to our own unique personhood.

We thus have the paradoxical situation that, even in this world, the important things are not political, even though the political is worthy. But it is more of a servant than an end. It is no accident that Christ came to redefine the exercise of political authority as a service to others, not as an exaltation of one's own power or glory. Politics makes real goods possible but does not constitute them. It provides a way or an arena for them to come forth. But it cannot substitute for them or the activities that flow from the individual person. Each existing person is a new reflection of reality. The state does not cause this newness or its energy but depends on them.

As it has the power of coercion, the state has a potentially dangerous relation to human goods if it goes awry.

Coercion is itself a necessity in many instances when wrong actions need to be confronted and dealt with. In itself, coercion or force is not evil. It is designed to keep unreasonable actions within the polity under control so that reason and law may rule there. Much evil is caused by the wrong use of force but also by not using force at all when needed. Not all men at all times act reasonably.

Politics does not look to the utopian idea of eliminating all evil but to the practical arrangement in which it can be contained, limited, and used for a valid purpose. The prevalence of evil means that, in all actual regimes, human beings who act unreasonably are found. They are real human beings, however, whose final fate is still the condition and purpose of their existence. Fallen man is still redeemed man. Evil is not the last word in a world within which reason, repentance, and forgiveness are possible.

Christian revelation teaches that Christ came to save sinners, that is, finite human beings who are not perfect. He came to save ordinary, limited, sinful human beings. If Greek philosophy seems designed for the elite, the more perfect, then Christian revelation is designed for those ordinary people whose lives are anything but perfect. This emphasis is probably why Chesterton said that Christianity is democratic in its scope. By this he meant that the life that God gave to each person at his very conception is the life that, in spite of its subsequent sins and faults, Christ sought to redeem and save, as it were, in spite of itself.

This recognition of the ordinary limitations of ordinary men is not an argument against the good or better human beings who manage to be more virtuous. It is an argument on behalf of those who do not always lead commendable lives but, at some point, would like to. Revelation is designed to provide a way to save those who would not be saved without it. That effort is the great initiative of the divine mercy toward us. In all probability because of our freedom, it is not always successful, hence the need for judgment.

V

The earthly city, as I use the term here, refers to the actual civil societies of human history, however they be structured, whatever they be called, whenever they exist. By the term, I intend to include all human beings who have ever been conceived and existed in this world. Augustine also uses the term "city of man" to refer not so much to earthly cities but to that city inhabited by those who definitively chose to reject God's grace and love, always a possibility open to a free creature. In this sense, the Roman Empire is an earthly city, not the "city of man", though symbolically it is sometimes called that even in Scripture and acts on the side of the Devil. I will approach what I want to say here through a famous passage in the Vatican II document *Gaudium et Spes*, the Pastoral Constitution on the Church in the Modern World.[7]

The first sentence in paragraph 22 reads: "The truth is that only in the mystery of the incarnate Word does the mystery of man take on light." Blessed John Paul II, in his first encyclical, *Redemptor Hominis*, spelled out the significance of this sentence. It acknowledges that we will not completely understand what man really is, not completely know ourselves, by our own scientific or philosophic methods,

---

[7] The quotes in the following paragraphs are from *Gaudium et Spes*, 22.

though they do tell us something. At first sight, this will seem to be a blow to human autonomy, but its effect is not to lessen human dignity but to make it more profound.

To see what is at issue, we first need to understand something of Christ in the Incarnation. We cannot know ourselves until we know who and what Christ is. Christ reveals what man is by becoming man Himself. He explains man to himself. This reality implies that man is more than himself. He cannot explain himself to himself by himself. Though he is a real agent, he is not a self-creator, however much he is tempted to think that he is. Something surrounds him that is beyond the merely human. He is in fact created not to be merely human but to be more than human. *Homo non proprie humanus sed superhumanus est.* This inner core of his being explains why he is never satisfied with the goods, power, or glory that he initially thinks will satisfy him. He is intrinsically incapable of resting in anything less than that for which he is created. This internal unrest, as Augustine suggested in his famous quote, "Our heart is restless until it rests in You", is in fact a blessing. It prevents us from finally confusing a false end with the true one.

Personal self-reflection shows that we do not fully know ourselves. What is our origin? What is our purpose? Who, then, is Christ if He is necessary to explain us to ourselves? He is, to cite Colossians, "the image of the invisible God" (Col 1:15). He is the "Son of Man" of whom the Hebrew prophets spoke. Christ constantly speaks to "*His* Father". He does not call Him, as He teaches us to do, "*our* Father". To Christ, He is "*My* Father". He says that He and the Father are one, as if it is the most obvious thing in the world (Jn 10:30). He says that He who has seen Him has seen the Father (Jn 14:8–9). He chides one of the apostles for not knowing this.

These are Trinitarian references to the inner life of the Godhead. They speak of a relation that has nothing to do with created things but has everything to do with the reality within divine things. Christ is also the perfect man. He is both God and man. This is the great blasphemy for the Jews and unbelievers, not that God is God, but that a true man is God. The understanding of this truth depends on the proper distinctions being made. It is only blasphemy if it is not true, if evidence for its truth were not in place. A man known in history states implicitly that He is God with the powers of God. He comes to restore in each of us what was lost from the first sin in Adam, something that perplexes us in each of our lives, something we have to deal with all the time.

"There are men who want to live a good life and have already decided to do so, but are not capable of bearing sufferings even though they are ready to do good", Augustine writes.[8]

> Now it is part of the Christian's strength not only to do good works but also to endure evil. Weak men are those who appear to be zealous in doing good works but are unwilling or unable to endure the sufferings that threaten. Lovers of the world, however, who are kept from good works by some evil desire, lie sick and listless, and it is this sickness that deprives them of any strength to accomplish good works.

When Christ became man, He did good works and endured evil. His human nature was true and complete. He is true God and true man but one Person. Technically put, Christ was not a human person but a divine one. His human actions

---

[8] Augustine, *On Pastors* (*Sermo 46*), 13, in the Liturgy of the Hours, Office of Readings, Twenty-Fifth Sunday in Ordinary Time, Second Reading, 4:285–86.

were ultimately rooted in His being within the Godhead. This source is why He can reveal God to us. He was a divine Person. All in Him was unified. He restored the doing of good works and the enduring of evil that directed us to the transcendent life for which we were created.

By His Incarnation, "the Son of God has united Himself in some fashion with every man." The implications of this sentence are sweeping. "Every man" means here every man, woman, and child who ever existed in any place or condition. This is a transcendent claim, for it links each existing person with an origin and an end in the Godhead. It unites every actual member of the human race in history into one destiny. This linkage is the ultimate source of our highest dignity. Thus, we can say that Christ had the same human nature that the rest of us have. We are invited to be adopted sons of God, that is, to live after our manner the gift of the divine nature. Christ is united with us as we are united with everyone else through our similarity in being what we are. We are certain kinds of beings, human beings. We are unique to ourselves.

Even more is implied here. The Incarnation is described in John's Prologue as "the Word became flesh" (Jn 1:14). That is, the Person in the Trinity known as the Word, the only-begotten Son, true God of true God, became man. This Word was in the beginning. None of the other individuals of the human race were in existence in the beginning. However, they were, in another sense, known in God as capable of being created. Each is a reflection, an image, of a truth within the Godhead. When they come to be in this world through their own conception and birth, they each betray origins from beyond this world. This is why we ourselves can never completely fathom another human being. He is fully known only to God.

Was this Christ truly man? "He worked with human hands, He thought with a human mind, acted by human choice and loved with a human heart." His two natures, divine and human, were not mixed. He was not a kind of hybrid of God and man. The two natures did not operate against one another but were unified in one Person. This Christ was innocent of sin. Yet He stood in our place before the Father. He made our way to the Father open again by His blood. We are reconciled to God in Christ. We can all say properly that God "loved me". He provided us an example of how to live. Christ is called the second Adam. He is the one who repairs at its root the disorder of the first Adam. Christ does this restoring by suffering the consequences of our sins while not Himself sinning.

We are able to obey and follow the New Law, the law of love, because of His grace. It is the Spirit, present at Jesus' conception, that raised Jesus from the dead. He has promised the same for us. "Death shall have no dominion." Christ's Resurrection is primarily not for Himself but for us, that we might finally be what we are intended to be in our creation, something that involves our free acceptance. We still have many trials and sufferings. These still lead to death and resurrection. They are not in vain, unless we make them so, as we can.

The document continues: "All this holds true not only for Christians, but for all men of good will in whose hearts grace works in an unseen way." Again, this is a striking passage. Much goes on in this world of which we are not aware. What holds true for all men of goodwill, not just Christians? What holds true is that each existing person is created by God for His purpose in order that each person may be happy, which includes the resurrection of his body. Each is redeemed by Christ—no exceptions. We can only speculate how this grace comes about for those who do not directly know Him. The Spirit is at work without restriction of national boundaries or time.

From the divine side, everything is in place to save everyone, if he will it. Each person is to undergo death and eventual resurrection. Salvation is possible. But the vale of tears remains our normal lot in the earthly city. The only way to return to God is through Christ, who has redeemed us with His blood. Our sins and disorders remain our own. They do not disappear simply because we know our condition. They need to be accounted for, forgiven. But provision for their forgiveness is included in the Church. This is why Christ came among us. The Holy Spirit in a manner known only to God, moreover, "offers to every man the possibility of being associated with this paschal mystery". Many have tried to propose other ways of salvation. It seems almost necessary that they do if they reject the Christian one. Yet, what remains certain is that no other way exists but that "associated with the paschal mystery".

Christ died to redeem each human person whether he accepts the sacrifice or not. "The ultimate vocation of man is in fact one, and divine." That is, only one proper description of our lot can be found. Redemption is not, as it were, multicultural, but transcultural. The many descriptions of other ways are shadows or errors in comparison. The mystery is a "great one". The "riddles of sorrow and death" become meaningful in Christ. Apart from this explanation, we are overwhelmed with the insufficiency of other ways. Life is "lavished" on us. The life we are given and created for is in fact eternal life, not simply mortal life. We are now able to say "Abba", that is, that God is our Father. This is how Christ addressed Him, evidently because it speaks what He is.

Our lives in our respective earthly cities, then, are passing lives. For a good part of the human race that has already existed, life is passed. Each person now dead has reached his judgment and lives in it. The judgment is the result of the actual life each person has lived. The scope of what we speak of here is vast. To know this breadth is a "reasonable pleasure". It explains much about us that we wonder about and need to know. We should not forget, however, that the grandeur of the cosmos is not apart from the drama of man's existence within it. In a real sense, the story of the universe is subsequent to the story of man, even though the universe is there first in time. Such reflections bring us to the final two chapters, on worship, our stance to God within the cosmos, and on eternal life, the purpose for which we are created.

CHAPTER 7

WORSHIP

"As to your employment in a future state, the sacred writers say little. The Revelation, however, of St. John gives us many ideas, and particularly mentions musick." JOHNSON. "Why, Sir, ideas must be given you by means of something which you know: and as to musick there are some philosophers and divines who have maintained that we shall not be spiritualized to such a degree, but that something of matter, very much refined, will remain. In that case, musick may make a part of our future felicity."

— Boswell's Life of Johnson[1]

Sing praises to the LORD, who dwells in Zion! Tell among the peoples his deeds!

—Psalm 9:11

Such are the consequences which naturally follow, when, from one cause or other, any of those doctrines is obscured, which have been revealed in mercy to our necessities. The mind catches the words of life, and tries to apprehend them, and being debarred their true meaning, takes up with this

---

[1] James Boswell, *Boswell's Life of Johnson*, Saturday, March 27, 1772 (London: Oxford University Press, 1931), 1:447.

or that form of error, as the case may be, in the semblance
of truth, by way of compensation.

—John Henry Newman, "The Gift of the Spirit" [2]

I

Though this chapter on worship follows that on the earthly
city, in another sense, it relates back to the chapter on sports
and play. Something delightful strikes our mind, our reason, when we realize that, in our experience, in our deep
fascination with a game or a drama, we touch on what
approaches the divine. This fascination is something that is
what it is, that does not interest us for anything other than
itself, for *what it is, that it is.* We again experience the surprisingly "reasonable pleasure" that things do fit together.
They are not groundless, and we are not clueless. We read
of wisdom: "I was daily his [the Lord's] delight, rejoicing
before him always" (Prov 8:30).[3] How lovely that is! And
in Psalm 96, we read: "Let the heavens be glad, and let the
earth rejoice; let the sea roar, and all that fills it; let the
field exult, and everything in it! Then shall all the trees of
the wood sing for joy" (vv. 11–12). Such imagery reminds
us that something more than mechanics is going on in our
cosmos. Somehow an appropriate response rises forth because

[2] John Henry Newman, "The Gift of the Spirit", in *Parochial and Plain
Sermons* (1891; San Francisco: Ignatius Press, 1987), 647.
    [3] The famous song-hymn "Morning Has Broken" by Eleanor Farjeon,
used in Morning Prayer for Wednesday of the First Week of the psalter in
the Liturgy of the Hours, contains these words: "Mine is the sunlight! / Mine
is the morning, / Born of the one light / Eden saw play!" Liturgy of the Hours,
3:748.

of the very existence of things, as if somehow thanks are due to someone for *all that is*.

The image here is that all of creation is related to God, not after the manner of some necessity or duty, but, after first beholding Him, then in response to Him, by rejoicing before the Lord as a delighted reaction to what is really there. Such is our reaction to the wonder of what is there, of *what is*. It is, likewise, almost as if God Himself is fascinated with His own creation and with what goes on within it. Well, no doubt, He is. That is what we call providence, the order of things outside the Godhead under His guidance to the end for which we were created in the first place. This is why we need to know what this end is and why; as Aquinas said, God saw fit to reveal it to us, lest we be confused.

Chesterton, in *The Everlasting Man*, put it slightly differently but made the same point: "The more deeply we think of the matter, the more we shall conclude that, if indeed there be a God, his creation could hardly have reached any other culmination than the granting of a real romance to the world." [4] I can think of no other reason but this romance as to why God would really be incited to create the world in the first place. No better reason is possible or desired. And in all romances, we find risk, even the risk of God. God Himself has to let free creatures be free. That is His risk; otherwise, the response of finite beings to Him would be meaningless. We find this risk at the center of our lives. It is why human lives are so dramatic from God's point of view.

The need of redemption follows from the fact that God risked the possibility of men's rejecting Him by creating

---

[4] G. K. Chesterton, *The Everlasting Man* (San Francisco: Ignatius Press, 1993), 380.

them free. God is, consequently, concerned with the sins of men and how they deal with them. It is rather like the way cheating and breaking the rules are related to games. Even sins, as was hinted in Tolkien's *Silmarillion*, become part of the "great dance".[5] They finally give a reflected glory. The freedom in the world that makes our sins possible increases, not lessens, God's interest in the world, in how to deal with fallen men. The central issue in the human worship of God is based on God's own free response to human sin in time.

Aristotle compared sports and play to contemplation. He was struck by the fact that games are for their own sake. They were like contemplation except that their subject matter was not so serious. The word *serious* as used in respect to God is Platonic. So is the word *unserious*, when used in respect to everything else.[6] Only God is serious, as Plato said in his *Laws*.[7] All else, though delightful, is by comparison unserious. Aristotle, in his *Ethics*, noticed that people eat, cough, and whisper in a play when they lose interest in it.[8] When they are gripped with music or plot or action, they are silent, in awe. Evidently, what was "serious" could be imitated in a way by the things that we play at or in the dramas that we enact. Most of us have such experiences of being drawn outside of ourselves in watching games or sitting in a concert hall or theater. Ultimate things pass before us as we watch. We can reflect God not only in our being His images but in our doing and making.

---

[5] C. S. Lewis, *Perelandra* (New York: Macmillan, 1965), 214.

[6] See James V. Schall, *On the Unseriousness of Human Affairs* (Wilmington, Del.: ISI Books, 2001).

[7] Plato, *Laws*, 803c, in *Plato, Complete Works*, ed. John M. Cooper (Indianapolis: Hackett, 1997).

[8] Aristotle, *Ethics*, bk. 10, 1175b10–15.

Both theater and games have two sides, the participating in them and the beholding of them. We are, as we said earlier (chapter 4), beings who receive things, including our own being. Hence, we have the power of acting according to our being. What I want to affirm in this chapter is that the proper worship of God is likewise something that we receive. We must also freely will to accept it as a gift, for it comes to us in no other form. A gift that need not be given or accepted. In many ways, the spirit of proper worship is closer to the beholding of what takes place in games and theater than to the participation in them. Such worship is of serious and solemn import. Like wisdom "playing before" the Lord.

Of the Ten Commandments, the first three have to do with our relation to God, which is what worship is about. If we be sane, we do not worship ourselves, though not everyone seems to know this. The first commandment identifies the god whom we worship as the God of Abraham, Isaac, and Jacob. The first commandment distinguishes the God whom we are to worship from all other gods. Evidently, false gods can everywhere be found, a subject, as Newman hinted above, of vast import. Indeed, much of human history is bound up with the worship of false gods and its consequences, which are often political. The knowledge of "false gods" and studies of them are ever-vital enterprises for seekers of truth.

The state, likewise, has rather too often put itself in the place of God. A concern of God Himself, for the sake of our being, is that He be worshipped in a proper way, after the manner most fitting for His own being. The reason for this divine concern is not that somehow God can be injured by false worship but that human beings can be and are so injured. If we worship God wrongly, we will not understand ourselves or the world properly. That we ought to understand the world and the cosmos properly is what human intelligence is about.

The second commandment tells us not to take the name of God in vain. Aristotle had remarked that nature produces nothing "in vain", that is, without a proper purpose.[9] The second commandment is not just talking about cuss words. To take the name of the Lord in vain means that we consciously or implicitly deny Him His due. We are untruthful about His presence in creation. We confuse creature and God. Our mind does not conform to reality. The name of God is itself something that we discover from revelation, the "I AM WHO I AM" of Exodus (Ex 3:14). By our own powers, we cannot name the essence of God. All the many other names we give Him are analogies or images based on something we know of His effects in things. The name of a thing represents *what it is*. We want to name God as He has named Himself. This proper naming is the only way we can speak accurately of Him. But that God could tell us His name and we could receive it are testimonies to the power of reason in which we are created in the first place.

The third commandment tells us to keep holy the Sabbath day. Clearly, it is possible for us to profane it. We do this profanation, presumably, by not doing what the Lord asked of us for this day, as well as by not living virtuous lives. What constitutes the holiness of this day? Wisdom "plays before the Lord" (see Prov 8:30). This image touches on the spirit of worship. That is the basic meaning of the Last Supper and its consequences. *Holy* is the word that

---

[9] Aristotle, *Politics*, 1253a9, in *Basic Works of Aristotle*, ed. Richard McKeon (New York: Random House, 1941).

surrounds God—"Holy, holy, holy", as we read in Isaiah (Is 6:3). We are to worship God not only by words and deeds but "in spirit and truth" (Jn 4:23). Peter confesses of Christ: "You are the Holy One of God" (Jn 6:69). The day we set aside for worship becomes a day of our freedom from all else that is less important, however pressing. By this very fact, it also becomes a day in which we can look again at the important things of God, even at ourselves and those we love.

In worship, both our external and internal being is involved. The whole drama of the prophet Ezekiel was that we be not held collectively responsible for the sins of our fathers. We each are held responsible by God for our own deeds. This principle of our own responsibility remains true of our worship. It is why we say in the Creed: "I believe . . ." We belong to each of those who recite the same words with the same meaning. No collective being exists apart from the individual persons who can attest to their particular belief, who can articulate it, sing it, affirm "I believe" and then state what it is that is believed. We do not just "believe". We believe in this, in that, in "God, the Father almighty . . ."

II

In the background of the worship of God is the classical virtue known as piety. Virgil's hero Aeneas was known as *pius Aeneas*. Piety was considered to be an aspect of the virtue of justice. Justice meant to render to each what is due. In the case of justice, this what-was-owed was usually clear, even mathematical. In the case of piety, what was owed was not so easily understood. Piety was concerned with the answer to the question: Is there in justice anything that is due to our parents or to the gods? After all, they gave us life and being, even without our asking. Piety is thus considered to be a natural, not a supernatural, virtue. We could manage to figure out on our own that we owe something to the gods.

Roman and Greek societies had their own civic "liturgies" that endeavored to fulfill this evident obligation of returning at least something to the gods. Civil theology regulated this form of worship. Obviously, everyone understood that more or less appropriate forms could be established. All these forms were designed to reflect what a people held the gods to be and how a people viewed their relation to them. Some forms of worship were in practice lofty, others degrading. The Romans found a niche in their Pantheon for all the gods of the peoples that they conquered, as if to claim that all gods belonged under the Roman gods. They had to leave the niche for the Hebrew God empty, as the Hebrews' God had no graven image. The Roman solution to leave the shrine empty was rather profound in its own way.

Just what would be pleasing to the gods, however, was not clear. Is it possible to be obliged to something that cannot be specifically defined? Even more, is it possible to return something appropriate to the gods, who gave us everything? They themselves evidently need nothing. What do we have to give them? This is the issue of things beyond justice, yet it has its roots in justice. The world would be a terrible place without justice. Likewise, it would be a terrible place if only justice existed. *Fiat justitia, pereat mundum!*—Let justice be done, even if the world perishes! Yet, though we cannot do everything, we should do something. Even so, the something that we finally do is not necessary to the gods.

As we noted above, piety indicated that something was owed to the gods. But it was not quite clear what was to be done. The history of man's religions indicates that many and varied efforts were devised to figure out just in what this pious duty consisted. Things like the sacrifice of first-fruits, or animals, or even human sacrifices; libations, incantations, dances, silences—hundreds of such efforts are known. Anthropology is full of their descriptions. These attempts even suggest that making some effort to please the gods is essential to human nature as it actually has existed over time. In this sense, we can distinguish between the sense that we do owe something to the gods and just what it is we do in particular to express our efforts to honor them. The former seems to be universal; the latter, the particular rites, varies from time to time and from place to place. Their description constitutes the history of natural religion. The sense that we owe something to the gods is natural law; the way in which this is rendered is positive law.

Christianity is not a natural religion. Indeed, it is difficult to say that it is a religion at all in the strict sense. If it has a position about the worship of God, which it does, it is because the form and nature of that worship was contained in its basic revelation that it received through the Old Testament and then through the life of Christ and the Church. The fact that a proper way to worship God was contained in revelation does not mean that the human effort to express this duty was wrong or ill-tempered. It was in principle a good thing, though some of the rites were in fact dangerous or evil—ritual human sacrifice, prostitution, or human exploitation.

Nor is the human participation in the Christian liturgy or rite, though it also requires grace, an absolute subjection

to the overpowering majesty of Allah, as in the Muslim
concept of worship. There man is completely passive, even
to the extent of denying any secondary causality on the
part of man or the cosmos out of fear of lessening the divine
omnipotence by suggesting that something else in the world
does something besides Allah. God becomes simply pure
will that can do and in fact does the opposite of whatever
He wants. In this sense, nothing is stable. All can be otherwise, including the commandments. The logic of this occa-
sionalist view ultimately is that neither we nor the world is
necessary or has any real purpose. The reason why God
might act outside of Himself, namely that finite beings might
respond to Him in freedom and love, is denied in the name
of Allah's complete domination of everything. All motion
is thus attributed to Allah, not to the being that is not God.
This too is why, in the Muslim paradise, even Allah himself
seems to be missing. All that is left is an idealized enjoyment of what are essentially earthly delights with no proper
object of vision given to the human powers as their proper
end.

From a Christian point of view, it stands to reason that
the proper worship of God could not be something exclu-
sively developed by human beings, but neither could it
neglect them. Paul thus wrote to the Ephesians:

> Blessed be the God and Father of our Lord Jesus Christ,
> who has blessed us in Christ with every spiritual blessing in
> the heavenly places, even as he chose us in him before the
> foundation of the world, that we should be holy and blame-
> less before him. He destined us in love to be his sons through
> Jesus Christ, according to the purpose of his will, to the
> praise of his glorious grace which he freely bestowed on us
> in the Beloved. In him we have redemption through his
> blood, the forgiveness of our trespasses. (Eph 1:3–7)

Thus, it would be fitting, after the implications of the Incarnation itself, to involve men in some manner in the rite of worship, including their creativity, language, and speech.

But lacking this divine guidance, it was proper in ancient times to do what seemed reasonable or worthy. In fact, the timing of revelation, if we might put it that way, recalling what was just cited from Paul, seems to have been such that it allowed mankind to see what it would develop by itself. Men would see finally that they could not fully fulfill their duty in piety by themselves. This too is a "rational pleasure". There would be no reason, moreover, why some of these pagan rites or practices could not be purified and reordered into a proper form of worship. Christianity did this adaptation from its beginning and still seeks to do so in its missionary work, even in the modern world. But the core of the revelation and of the liturgy remains: "God is God." His inner life is the what-is-outside-of-ourselves to which we are drawn by our very being because it is the "I AM WHO I AM".

This background allows us to speak of a supernatural piety, a due worship of God that is worthy of both man and God. In one sense, it seems paradoxical to suggest that the proper human worship of God is something that has to be supplied by God Himself. This view might tend to make God "antihuman" or infinitely aloof, as most classical, oriental, and modern religions often indicate. This difficulty, of course, the distance between man and God, is what the Incarnation is about. In that sense, the Incarnate Person is both man and God, or the man-God. His life and death, in liturgical celebration, is the proper focus of the human worship of God. It is the Mass that is the proper worship of God. Present, as the rite specifically says, are not only those there but the very Trinity itself, the choirs of heaven, the saints, the souls of purgatory, the living and the dead. The phrase "cosmic liturgy" for the Mass is quite right. Each Mass intends to direct all of creation back to the Father through the Son and the Spirit in the awe of the Father's glory. Nothing less.

In her book *After Writing*, Catherine Pickstock argued that the classical Roman rite of the Mass embodied the most perfect form of worship of God.[10] One can compare the many rites that exist and have existed in the history of the Church, their language, music, structure, wordings, and movements. If they be orthodox, the combination of word, sacrifice, and communion will be present. The Mass, in its essence, is the same sacrifice of the Cross that Christ endured. It embodies the whole Trinitarian life as it came to be present among us in the life and death of Christ, in His passing on to the Church the office of doing these things in remembrance of Him.

When the Church came to answer the question of how to observe the third commandment about keeping holy the Sabbath—now, on account of the Resurrection, to be held on Sunday—she insisted on the attendance of the faithful at Mass. This rite is the Church's answer to the question of piety, to how we are to fulfill our obligations to God, though it includes our striving to live a virtuous and repentant life of justice and charity. For this reason, we can speak of a "supernatural" piety.

The question of what is it that we owe to God is taken out of our hands but, at the same time, given back to us in the form of the memorial of Christ's death, Resurrection,

---

[10] Catherine Pickstock, *After Writing: On the Liturgical Consummation of Philosophy* (Oxford: Blackwell, 1998), 171ff.

and ascension. The external form of the Mass can be more or less elaborate. In language, in music, in speaking, in silences, in walking ritual, in vestments, in buildings and altars, the Mass can vary, yet it maintains the same essential function of being at a place where the action going on is to remember and make present the life and death of Christ. It affirms who He was. He returns to the Father.

Why, we might ask, would God go to the trouble of informing us how to worship Him properly? The Eucharist is the keeping present in the world the one action by which we are redeemed, the one action that, at the same time, is in the world and transcends it because of who and what Christ is, true God and true man.[11] It sums up what we are, what God is, how we stand to one another. So the essential issue is, why, having once created us, would God go to the trouble of redeeming us? Even more surprising, why did He go about redeeming us in the way that He did, by the Cross?

The Greeks already knew with Sophocles that "man learns by suffering", and with Socrates that "it is better to suffer evil than to do it." Revelation, as it expanded, was addressed initially to the Greek world, to people who already knew things that the poets and philosophers knew. What they did not yet know was the connection between their suffering, their salvation, and the eternal destiny of each. This is what Christ came to tell them. Not everyone, as far as we can tell, was willing to listen, even to today.

The Eucharist, cast in the form of the Last Supper, is the institution of the Mass as we know and commemorate it.

---

[11] See the remarkable essays on the Eucharist in Robert Sokolowski, *Christian Faith and Human Understanding* (Washington, D.C.: Catholic University of America Press, 2006), 69–150.

This is the form of worship that has existed in the world since the moment of its institution, now carried on by those whom Christ commissioned to commemorate Him in the Church. This is why one of the principal purposes of the Church is to make available, to make present, the sacraments in the world as Christ has indicated to her, particularly the Eucharist. This perfect praise of God is to be heard in all places and at all times.

The Church conceives the Mass to be going on in the world someplace at all hours so that a constant worship of the Father is being offered. This worship is, as it were, what holds the world together. What is being offered is the same sacrifice that the Son endured on the Cross, again the Redemption whereby we were saved. The priests and the Church are not themselves originators of this form of worship. They are present not in their own names. The priest acts "in the Person of Christ", not in his own name. Priests are not actors. The priest is to report and to enact what is handed down, not his own private opinions or innovations. He is always to be someone who is sent, not someone who is making up something new or from his own designs. We can go to Mass because Christ is there, not because we want to hear someone's opinions about what God might like us to do.

III

The proper worship of God is found in a specific, divinely revealed rite directed through the Church as the locus of its taking place. But attending a rite is not all there is to an ongoing human life, though that is its heart. The Church does not recommend that we be present at Mass all day, every day. Indeed, the requirement of attending Mass on Sunday, really a day of rest in the most profound sense, is rather a mild one in comparison with other forms of natural piety in other religions and cultures. The reason for this brevity has to do with the relation of everything else to worship. "Seek first his kingdom and his righteousness, and all these things shall be yours as well" (Mt 6:33).

If we get our priorities wrong, we will get our world wrong. Belloc once remarked that the world's greatest spiritual invention was the twenty-minute daily morning Mass that a man could attend and thence go out about his work, which was also essential to his earthly and even spiritual life and final destiny. The worship of God, in other words, is connected with everything else that we do. Indeed, we might say that Christianity intends to incorporate everything into the worship of God by seeing *what it is* and allowing it to be *what it is*. All things are good in their proper order. *Omne ens est bonum et verum*—every being is both good and true.

During the Reformation, a controversy with Luther arose about whether the term *vocation* was limited to the religious and vowed life in the Church. From the very beginning of Christianity, of course, the family was considered to be even a "domestic church". The events that transpired in the family already reached eternity in the weddings, births, sicknesses, joys, and deaths of its members. However, the worship of God also includes love of neighbor outside the family and the carrying out, in the earthly city, of the normal affairs of mortal men. This understanding of a proper vocation, or "calling", for every worthy way of life is generally accepted today.

Throughout the letters of Paul and the readings of the Fathers of the Church, moreover, we see constant reference to the fact that the worship of God involves our own souls, how we rule ourselves, as Aristotle would have it. We are to worship in spirit and in truth. We are responsible also for one another as well as ourselves. Our actions are real, and they have consequences.

We are not mere "occasions" of submission to divine action. We are not philosophical idealists for whom matter does not count. We are not to be ourselves unworthy. That is to say, the very notion of the worship of God includes the right ordering of the human soul before both God and men, the calling of each person to what he is created to be, the awareness that we are not "of ourselves" alone.

The motto of the Order of Saint Benedict is *Ora et labora*, "Pray and work"; that of the Order of Saint Dominic, along with *Veritas*, "Truth", is *Contemplata aliis tradere*, "To give to others the fruits of contemplation"; and that of the Society of Jesus is *In actione contemplativus*, "Contemplation in action". By calling these phrases to mind, I want next to consider how it is possible to look on the world and ourselves as engaged in the worship of God in all we do. Moreover, what really matters is not just that our actions have some effect and worth but that their very being, by being what they are, is also a worship of God.

Paul did not tell us to "pray constantly", for nothing (1 Thess 5:17). We are to go about this praying always in such a way that the relative autonomy of this world remains what it is and that what we are supposed to do gets done. Our prayer and our deeds are not to be absorbed into some pantheistic or voluntarist vortex that leaves our loves and deeds emptied of any individual reality by substituting God for His creation.

In Christianity, God is not "part" of the world. He transcends it. Though the world need not be, God nevertheless created it with the levels of being within it as themselves good. We acquire the final and clearest orientation of our lives from the Mass, from the "following of Christ", to cite the title of what is perhaps the most widely read Christian book after the Bible.[12] The worship of God does not, in spite of the Marxist claims to the contrary, lessen our appreciation for things of this world but in fact enhances it once we know that all being is good. God looked on His creation, it says in Genesis, and saw that it was *good*.

The greatest enemy of God, the heresy of the Manicheans of all ages, is the claim that matter is not good. Thus, the worship of God heightens our appreciation of what need not exist but does. It puts the finite things of reality in order. We know that they are, but also that they are not God. Reflection on these classic mottos of the religious orders will, I think, be quite insightful for us to see how worship of God in its fullness is in everything we do. Indeed, in this endeavor, we again find a rational pleasure, some insight into the fact that things cohere, some delight that they do and that we see how it is possible.

Most people know that, within the Church, almost from her beginning, many good people seemingly fled from the world as a dangerous place for a spiritual and edifying life. Chesterton wrote about this background in his book *St. Francis of Assisi*. Somehow, the things of the body, not without the help of some elements in Platonic philosophy, seemed to contaminate things. No one who has read the New Testament, moreover, can really doubt that the world is also viewed as a dangerous place. The term *world*, however, can mean the very cosmos itself, which is good and to be praised.

---

[12] *The Following of Christ* (1418), also known as *The Imitation of Christ*, by Thomas à Kempis.

This is the world we encounter, the world science investigates, the world with all its beauty and power.

But, especially in the apostle John's writing, *world* can also refer to all those things that are opposed to God. We are to recognize these opposed things, but not follow them. It is not a Christian virtue to underestimate the Devil and the power of evil among us to corrupt or deflect good things, including especially ourselves, from achieving their purpose. Our struggle is not against flesh and blood but "against the principalities, against the powers", as Saint Paul said (Eph 6:12).

In his essay "The Purpose of Politics", Josef Pieper wrote: "For it is contemplation that preserves in the midst of human society the truth which is at one and the same time useless and the yardstick of every possible use; so it is contemplation which keeps the true end in sight, gives meaning to every practical act of life." [13] This remarkable passage is based on the famous Greek distinction between the contemplative and the active life, a distinction that often came into Christianity via the contrast of Mary and Martha in the Gospel. It is the contemplation of *what is*, what exists for its own sake, that preserves among us that bright truth by which we can measure our thoughts and actions to decide whether they be good.

What Pieper rightly points out here is that we must also have those in our midst who are directly devoted to the worship of God in all their days, who devotedly keep the sense of the divine in our midst, whether we know it or not. Traditionally, in the Church, the contemplative religious orders—the Carmelites, the Cistercians, the Trappists—have specifically

---

[13] Josef Pieper, "The Purpose of Politics", in *Josef Pieper: An Anthology* (San Francisco: Ignatius Press, 1989), 123.

sought to fulfill this role. Lest we begin to think that this world is all there is, a very common modern temptation, we need witness to things of the highest moment, even midst the important, busy, and dangerous things of the world. We must keep the true end of our lives, eternal life itself, at least in sight. Such is the abiding witness of the contemplatives among us. "Man does not live by bread alone" is the famous way the same point is put in Scripture (Mt 4:4). Man must also live by seeking to see God, for this is ultimately why he was created, not only that he seeks but that he finds.

The Benedictine motto, the famous "Pray and work", from the early Middle Ages took up this issue of more organized and systematic contemplation. The monks of the West were not hermits. They lived together in community, a community centered on what came to be called "the work of God", the *opus Dei*. This arrangement meant that time began to be organized around the Mass and the hours of the Divine Office. At these times, God was specifically praised and worshipped. What about other times of the day? Was it also possible to "work" in the fields, in printing, building, or teaching? Or was prayer everything?

In the Greek world, much of the necessary work was done by slaves. Aristotle suspected that some relation existed between lack of technology and slavery. Was it possible to redeem slavery, however, by elevating the dignity of work? Work was considered menial and unworthy of cultivated man. With the new image of God doing His "work" of creation, why could not such enterprises as building cathedrals or roads, or caring for herds or the sick, be considered sanctifying? The work itself was worthwhile. Such things needed to be accomplished among us. The worker, the one who did the work, spent his time in the service of something that needed to be done for himself and others. It was worthwhile doing.

Generally speaking, a distinction existed between work that was servile and activities that were free or liberating, the servile arts and the liberal arts. Aristotle said that man is busy or works in order to be free to contemplate. The Dominican motto, *Contemplata aliis tradere*, to hand over to others what we have contemplated in our studies and meditations, came to terms with this issue.

The question was whether the combination of contemplation and handing over to others what we knew was better than contemplation alone, itself a high good. If the former was the case, the contemplative needed to go out from his cell into the world, where the people who needed to know live. This principle is implicit in the point of Pieper that we need in the midst of politics, the supreme human worldly activity, proper to man, as Aristotle said, those also who direct themselves primarily in the one thing necessary that is not, as such, political.[14]

Something in man transcends the world, good as the world is. If we do not have what transcends the world, then what happens is that politics or other activities become elevated in the place of God. It has happened again and again in the history of the world and happens even today, perhaps especially today. The earthly city has its place, but it is not the highest place. The Dominican principle sought to pass on knowledge of the highest things to others who had not the time or the inclination to devote to full-time contemplation. But the Dominicans understood that everyone both needed and wanted to know such things. They further maintained that it was possible to teach others and that this was a most noble enterprise. The highest things were essentially

---

[14] See also Josef Pieper, *Leisure: The Basis of Culture*, with a foreword by James V. Schall (1952; San Francisco: Ignatius Press, 2009).

open to everyone, free of charge, if we could but find those who would teach them to us.

The Jesuit motto, *In actione contemplativus*, "Contemplation in action", had a rather different focus, though this principle too depended on the contemplative heritage found in the Greeks, the Benedictines, and the Dominicans. We might even say it added the practicality and devotion to the poor of the Franciscans. In more recent centuries, many forms of what are called active religious life have been formed. Many had to do with education and health, others with aid to various groups of the poor or downtrodden.

In all cases, an impulse to aid or teach others was derived from the Christian principle that the love of God included, as a sign of its authenticity, the love of neighbor. We should never forget that the love of neighbor first consists in aiding him to see the highest of things. Christian evangelization is based on the fact that there are certain things each of us should know about God. Men need to know these things; someone must tell and teach them. Aquinas once said that the greatest thing we can do for our neighbor is to tell him the truth. The worship of God includes this truth and our pleasure in knowing it.[15]

[15] To the objection that telling others about the truth of Christianity is somehow against one's "freedom of religion", Benedict XVI, citing Paul VI (*Evangelii Nuntiandi*, 80), explained: "But to propose to their consciences the truth of the Gospel and salvation in Jesus Christ, with complete charity and with a total respect for the free openness which it presents—'without coercion, without unworthy or dishonorable pressure—far from being an attack on religious liberty is fully to respect that liberty, which is offered a choice of a way that even non-believers consider noble and uplifting. . . . The respectful presentation of Christ and His Kingdom is more than the evangelizer's right; it is his duty. It is likewise the right of his fellow men to receive from him the proclamation of the Good News of salvation.'" Benedict XVI, "Address to Bishops of Brazil", *L'Osservatore Romano*, English ed., October 23, 2010.

"Contemplation in action" comes from the *Spiritual Exercises* of Saint Ignatius. Roughly, this principle looks at the world as itself actively existing within the providence of God, which, of course, it does. Benedict XVI, in his English visit for the beatification of John Henry Cardinal Newman, said: "One of the Cardinal's best-loved meditations includes the words, 'God has created me to do him some definite service. He has committed some work to me which he has not committed to another.' " [16] This passage in Newman is exactly in the line of the Ignatian tradition.

The activity of God outside of Himself, the divine governance of the universe, goes on all the time and includes each of us in the drama by which we relate ourselves back to God. If this principle is true for Newman, then clearly it is true for everyone else. In that "everyone else", I would include every human being who ever existed in any form or place whether he died of old age or of abortion, whether he was a sinner or a saint. Every person exists for a work that is not committed to another. This was the same point that was made earlier in the discussion on hell about the radical significance of each of our lives and acts.

And this "contemplation in action" is not only the beholding of things in God's sustenance of them but our seeking to work out our salvation through guiding ourselves freely to choose and accept the end for which we are ultimately created, that is, "to praise, reverence, and serve" God, as Ignatius put it.[17] In this sense, we can say that there are two worlds. The first is simply the cosmos and its ongoing

[16] Benedict XVI, "Prayer Message in Hyde Park", *L'Osservatore Romano*, English ed., September 22, 2010. The Newman citation is from his *Meditations on Christian Doctrine*.

[17] Ignatius of Loyola, *The Spiritual Exercises of St. Ignatius*, trans. Louis J. Puhl, S.J. (Chicago: Loyola Press, 1968), 12.

development. But the second—the more important one, for the first exists for the second—is the world of human knowing, choice, and action, that which would not exist unless the rational creature existed within the cosmos itself both as a part of it and as what transcends it in each person born to everlasting life.

In the end, we can worship God in all things once we know what they are, once we know their origin and our purpose. But the proper way to worship God we must learn from God Himself. The wonder is not that we seek to know the highest things but that God Himself has taught us the proper worship, a worship that is centered on the Cross, the death, and the Resurrection of Christ, in the admonition to the apostles, "Do this in remembrance of me", that keeps it before us (Lk 22:19). No doubt, we will find those who maintain that it is "inhuman" or alienating to receive the way to worship God properly from God Himself. Such a view could be possible if we did not understand that the best things that we have, including the eternal life that is to be ours, are given to us.

We cannot achieve what is best for us only by ourselves, even when we must choose it when it is freely offered to us. When we look at it from this angle, I think it is proper to say that the worship of God is not only something we owe to God, but it is also a rational pleasure to see that the highest things are directed to our souls and that we can freely receive them in the generosity in which they are given to us. We can contemplate, work, pray, teach, know, and behold in all things the lively reality that we stand outside of nothingness.

We can see the wonder of what is there, a reality before which again we are to play, dance, sacrifice, and sing, as Plato too understood. The Church has preserved her rite of worship as her central point in this world. This is the point where the Incarnation and the Redemption remain among us, pointing to the Resurrection and the Trinity, because they are grounded in the man-God. He was born of woman in this world at a specific time and place. Each of us has something specific for which he is created. When, in our contemplations and actions, we see this purpose working itself in our lives, we do see the hand of God exactly where we are.

CHAPTER 8

ETERNAL LIFE

The seventh day will be our Sabbath, whose end will not be an evening, but the Lord's Day, an eighth day, as it were, which is to last for ever, a day consecrated by the resurrection of Christ, foreshadowing the eternal rest not only of the spirit but of the body also. There we shall be still and see; we shall see and we shall love; we shall love and we shall praise. Behold what will be, in the end, without end! For what is our end but to reach that kingdom which has no end?

—Augustine, *City of God*[1]

We must first consider what *eternal life* is. The thing to be noted is that in eternal life, man is united to God. God *Himself* is our reward and the end of all our labors.... Thus if we desire pleasure, there will be supreme and most perfect delight, in that its object will be God, the sovereign good.

—Thomas Aquinas, *Commentary on the Apostles' Creed*[2]

As we processed to the chancel at the beginning of this service, the choir sang that Christ is our "sure foundation".

[1] Augustine, *City of God*, trans. Henry Bettenson (Harmondsworth, England: Penguin, 2003), 20.30.

[2] Thomas Aquinas, *The Three Greatest Prayers: Commentaries on the Lord's Prayer, the Hail Mary, and the Apostles' Creed*, (Manchester, N.H., Sophia Institute Press, 2011), art. 13 (emphasis added).

He is the Eternal Son of God, of one substance with the
Father, who took flesh, as the Creed states, "for us men
and for our salvation". He alone has the words of everlasting life.

—Benedict XVI[3]

I

The worship of God is out-going. It celebrates what is there,
not of our own making. Psalm 89 reads: "I will sing of
your mercies, O Lord, for ever; with my mouth I will pro-
claim your faithfulness to all generations. For your merciful
love was established for ever, your faithfulness is firm as the
heavens" (vv. 1–2). Yet we wonder how this love, this faithfulness that we find in the heavens, comes back to us. We
are, on the surface, so mortal and finite. If we are to sing
forever of God's merciful love, does that not imply something about what we really are in the plan of God? In a
sense, to think we are merely finite and passing beings is an
illusion, even if that temporality is a stage and a reality that
we must hopefully enjoy or at least endure in our threescore
years and ten.

In Christian liturgical prayers, as well as in Scripture and
the writings of the Fathers of the Church, we often come
across the phrase *eternal life*. It provokes us. It even con-
founds us. We would not, perhaps, be so struck by it if it
applied only to God's life, which it primarily does. But

[3] Benedict XVI, "Introductory Words during the Evening Prayer", ecu-
menical celebration, Westminster Abbey, London, September 17, 2010, Holy
See website, www.vatican.va.

we cannot help but notice that it also everywhere is applied to us fragile human beings. We mortals, *we who die*, are promised and given personally, not collectively, eternal life! Indeed, strictly speaking, from the beginning, we are given no other kind of life. The so-called natural order, which is at least thinkable, never actually happened. A world in which man existed in his conceptual nature without grace never came forth, never was in God's plan for us. The race of men that we now know, the one to which we actually belong, from its inception, was created by God's plan and gift for something higher, not just for mortal life, but for *eternal life*.

The frequency with which we find the expression *eternal life*, or *everlasting life*, almost as a recurrent melody, surprises us. The last words of the Nicene Creed, to which Aquinas referred in the passage at the beginning of this chapter, read: *Et expecto resurrectionem mortuorum, et vitam venturi saeculi*—I expect the resurrection of the dead and life eternal in the age to come. This dogma—and it is that, to recall the first chapter—is responded to by those who hear and believe it. They say: "Amen—I concur." Here in eight Latin words, we affirm, *I affirm*, the truth of everything we would like to be true, even if we do not think it possible—the resurrection of our individual bodies and, what follows, eternal life. Such words recall the real objection to Catholicism, a theme on which this book is based. It is not that we are promised too little but that we are promised too much, too much for us to handle when we allow our minds to be narrow. We underestimate the reality, the will, and the power of God.

In the First Mass Preface on Weekdays in Ordinary Time, we read: "Therefore, He [Christ] was exalted above all creation and became the source of eternal life to all who serve Him." The Collect in the Mass of Friday, the Seventh Week of Easter, reads: "Father, in glorifying Christ and sending us your Spirit, you open the way to eternal life." The introductory antiphon to the Mass of Saints Simon and Jude on October 28 reads: "The Lord chose these holy men for their unfeigned love and gave them eternal glory."

In the breviary prayer after the Second Reading for Wednesday of the Thirty-First Week in Ordinary Time, we read: "May we live the faith we profess and trust your promise of eternal life."[4] A second-century homily, found in the breviary for Wednesday of the Thirty-Second Week in Ordinary Time, reads: "For the sake of eternal life, my brothers, let us do the will of the Father who called us, resisting the temptations that lead us into sin and striving earnestly to advance in virtue."[5] Finally, the Epistle to Titus begins: "Paul, a servant of God and an apostle of Jesus Christ, to further the faith of God's elect and their knowledge of the truth which accords with godliness, in hope of eternal life which God, who never lies, promised ages ago ..." (Tit 1:1–2). Such citations can be multiplied, but these are enough to emphasize their regular appearance in our prayers, teachings, and thinking.[6]

[4] Liturgy of the Hours, Office of Readings, Thirty-First Week in Ordinary Time, Wednesday, Prayer, 4:486.

[5] Ibid., Thirty-Second Week in Ordinary Time, Wednesday, Second Reading, 4:516.

[6] See Peter Kreeft, *Heaven: The Heart's Deepest Longing* (San Francisco: Ignatius Press, 1980); E. L. Mascall, *The Christian Universe* (London: Darton, Longman and Todd, 1966); Josef Pieper, *Hope and History* (San Francisco: Ignatius Press, 1994); Joseph Owens, *Human Destiny* (Washington, D.C.: Catholic University of America Press, 1985); and Kenneth Baker, "Heaven", in *Doctrinal Sermons on the Catechism of the Catholic Church* (South Bend, Ind.: St. Augustine's Press, 2012), 156–59.

II

Thus, in this final chapter, we pass from dogma, humor, play, hell, the earthly city, and the worship of God to our participation in the Trinitarian life itself. This Trinitarian life is that for which, ultimately, each of our kind is created. But, again, we receive it only if we will to accept it. It is offered, not forced, even after it is given to our nature, which itself needs to be prepared for it. The one unchanging principle of God in His dealing with our race in all its history from Adam is that God will not eradicate our freedom in order to give us His salvation. If salvation were not freely accepted, if it were accomplished in any other way, it would result in the lessening or losing of what we are because it would bypass our freedom. The whole point of creating the universe was, ultimately, the reciprocity of the love that bursts forth within the Godhead. The whole project of creation was premised on the fact that love must always be free, even in finite beings like us.

In the book of Wisdom, we read these remarkable words: "God did not make death, and he does not delight in the death of the living. For he created all things that they might exist, and the creatures of the world are wholesome.... For God created man for incorruption, and made him in the image of his own eternity, but through the devil's envy death entered the world" (Wis 1:13–14; 2:23–24). God did not make death. It was a result of the Fall, of choice. It was never intended to be among the race of Adam. But if death was caused by choice, it would have to be redeemed by choice and, indeed, by suffering. This, in brief, is the drama of the Incarnation.

Saint Ambrose, in his famous letter on the death of his brother, referred to by Benedict XVI in *Spe Salvi*, similarly writes:

Death was not part of nature; it became part of nature. God did not decree death from the beginning; he prescribed it as a remedy. Human life was condemned because of sin to unremitting labor and unbearable sorrow and so began to experience the burden of wretchedness. There had to be a limit to its evils; death had to restore what life had forfeited. Without the assistance of grace, immortality is more of a burden than a blessing.[7]

The notion of immortality without resurrection is a burden, as most classical literature hints. Death becomes rather a remedy to prevent this fate of endless misery from happening. The alternative to endless life of finite [or limited] beings is eternal life. It is this alternative that is, for human beings, the principal "rational pleasure" that comes from understanding what they, beings from the beginning ordered not just to mortality or immortality but to everlasting life. *Homo non proprie humanus sed superhumanus est*—Man properly speaking is not merely human but beyond the human. That principle is found in Aquinas' *De caritate* and used in E. F. Schumacher's brilliant book *A Guide for the Perplexed*.[8]

Near the beginning of his great encyclical *Spe Salvi*, Benedict XVI recalled something that startled me when I first read it. He was speaking of the baptism of infant children.

---

[7] Saint Ambrose, "From a Book on the Death of His Brother, Satyrus", in the Liturgy of the Hours, Office of Readings, All Souls' Day, November 2, Second Reading, 4:1539. Cited by Benedict XVI, *Spe Salvi* [Saved in hope] (Boston: Pauline Books, 2007), 10. Saint Ambrose also wrote: "The Lord allowed death to enter this world so that sin might come to an end. But he gave us the resurrection of the dead so that our nature might not end once more in death; death was to bring guilt to an end, and the resurrection was to enable our nature to continue for ever." "From a Treatise on Death as a Blessing", in the Liturgy of the Hours, Office of Readings, Thirty-First Week in Ordinary Time, Saturday, Second Reading, 4:498.

[8] E. F. Schumacher, *A Guide for the Perplexed* (New York: Harper Colophon, 1977).

I have baptized little children before. But I never particularly noticed what was being said. What drew my attention was that Benedict used a different phrase from that normally in our Roman Ritual though that phrase is there too as an alternative. He pictures parents bringing their newborn child to the baptismal font. Before he begins, the priest asks the parents the name of the child. Then he asks them what they want for their child. To this latter question, which is of such profound import, the answer in the ritual I usually use is "Faith", which is accurate enough. But the response Benedict selects is rather "Eternal life".[9] I confess that I was quite astounded to see, almost for the first time, that this was what parents wanted for their child at his baptism.

Benedict indicates that, at the baptism of their child, parents are concerned with the long run. They do not answer the question of what it is they want by responding "Looks", "Riches", "Fame", or even "Health". What they wish in faith, and why they are at the baptismal font, is that their child ultimately will have "eternal life", nothing less. The path to eternal life, as the Lord taught us, passes through baptism and, as Saint Ambrose said, through death. And this is what is revealed to us as the purpose of every human life, that it is created for eternal life. No higher dignity can be imagined. Little else matters.

Mothers and fathers here at the baptism of their child cut to the core of things. What they want for their child is precisely eternal life. One of the reasons that they are baptizing their child is so that he can also miss this life if he chooses to do so. So we have a double issue: (1) each of us is created to reach eternal life and live eternally; (2) we can

---

[9] Benedict XVI, *Spe Salvi*, 10.

miss the eternal life with the Trinity and continue in the alternate eternal life of possessing ourselves alone forever, which we usually call, as we have seen in chapter 5, hell.

For anyone with a soul not made of iron, the most startling, and yet the most welcome, passage in the New Testament, I sometimes think, is found at the end of the First Epistle of John. It reads: "And we know that the Son of God has come and has given us understanding, to know him who is true; and we are in him who is true, in his Son Jesus Christ. This is the true God and eternal life" (1 Jn 5:20). We know that "the Son of God has come". This knowing that a person calling Himself the Son of God has appeared among us is attested to as a fact, as Benedict argues, by all reasonable science and logic. Christ's reality is not presented as theory or myth, the two avenues so often used to avoid the fact of His having already come to dwell among us. It is presented as a real life, lived in a definite time and place, witnessed to by reputable sources and handed down to us reliably by the Church.[10]

This evidence and affirmation of the historic reality of Christ's coming comprised the essence of Benedict XVI's work *Jesus of Nazareth*.[11] The work established—and it is not the only one to do so—that, as far as all we know, Jesus Christ was and is the Son of Man, the "I AM", as He showed and maintained. He was sent into this world by His Father to redeem it. It does need redemption. He came at a specific time and place, which we can identify. This knowledge "has

[10] See Josef Pieper, *Tradition: Concept and Claim* (South Bend, Ind.: St. Augustine's Press, 2010). Chesterton's *Everlasting Man* is also well worth reading on this subject.

[11] Benedict XVI, *Jesus of Nazareth*, vol. 1, *From the Baptism in the Jordan to the Transfiguration* (New York: Doubleday, 2007); vol. 2, *Holy Week: From the Entrance into Jerusalem to the Resurrection* (San Francisco: Ignatius Press, 2011).

given us understanding", as John said in the quote above. He came so that we might know what is true of God and, indirectly, what is true of everything else, including ourselves. In Him is what is true. We are to be "in him". We are included in His life, death, and Resurrection.

The second from the last sentence of John's letter reads: *Hic est verus Deus, et vita aeterna*—This is the true God and eternal life. God is eternal life. This is one of the ways to describe Him. Life is identified with Him. He is its origin, always. What is more: This life is given to us, if we accept it. The key word is *given*. To accept it, we not only need to attend to the way we live while we are in time, but we need to attend to what is said to take the place of eternal life if this concept is rejected—continued life in this world, nothingness, souls without bodies. There is a logic to eternal life that brings together the very core and meaning of our lives.

To consider what eternal life might signify will, for many, seem to be odd, if not quaint. Surely it is mere empty speculation? Yet we constantly read in Christian revelation that it is for this purpose, eternal life, that each of us is created from nothing yet out of the abundance of God's love, power, and wisdom. Such is the real source of our actual life and being, of our restlessness and of our not feeling at home in this world. We need not exist but we are.

The Church exists, as Blessed John Paul II said, that we may know and remember these things: "The Church preserved within herself the memory of man's history from the beginning: the memory of his creation, his vocation, his elevation, and his fall. Within this essential framework, the whole of human history, the history of redemption is written." [12]

[12] John Paul II, *Memory and Identity* (New York: Rizzoli, 2005), 151.

Man's vocation, ultimately, is precisely eternal life. Our mortal life is the one first born and lived in this world. But ultimately, none of us has two lives, one in this world and one in the next. Each of us has but one life begun in this world at our conception and birth that is in fact eternal, however we choose to respond to the gift of this life that we find alive in our very being.

Aquinas defined time as *fluxus ipsius nunc*, that is, the ongoing flow of the now, in which we always find ourselves. We are always in a "now", a "present", but we know of tomorrow and yesterday. We have memory for what is past and hope for what is not yet. Aquinas also defined eternity as *nunc stans*, that "now" that stands, that is there. If we human beings did not exist in time, we could not be. Yet, in our music, in our philosophy, in our loves, and in our thought, we have intimations, hints, that time is not enough for us, even that we are not finally to rest in time, as if we did not already know that. T. S. Eliot, near the end of his "Dry Salvages", wrote:

> But you are the music / While the music lasts. These are only hints and guesses, / Hints followed by guesses; and the rest / Is prayer, observance, discipline, thought and action. / The hint half guessed, the gift half understood, is Incarnation.[13]

The issue has seldom been put more beautifully.

In Evelyn Waugh's final novel of his war trilogy *The Sword of Honour*, we read: "It was no good trying to explain, Guy [Couchback] thought. Had someone said: 'All differences are theological differences'? He turned once more to his father's letter: *Quantitative judgments don't apply. If only one soul was saved, that is full compensation for any amount*

---

[13] T. S. Eliot, "Dry Salvages", *Four Quartets* (New York: Harcourt, 1941), 4.44.

of 'loss of face.' "[14] Such a passage recalls what Benedict XVI cited from Newman, that some purpose is found in our lives that God wants each of us in particular, not in the abstract, to accomplish.[15] And the statement "All differences are theological differences" turns us back to the "rational pleasures" that run through these pages. The very intelligence that the essence of revelation incites in us is itself, on our part, a delight. We do hold things by faith, but this faith is grounded in everything we know to be true and enhances it.

III

A consideration of eternal life might, at first sight, seem to most people to be too esoteric, too peculiar to that band of believers who call themselves Catholic and Christian. It is noted that many of these same believers yield to the pressures, often from within the ranks of their clerical and intellectual dons, to transpose any notion of eternal life into a this-worldly project.[16] They insist on doubting

---

[14] Evelyn Waugh, *The End of the Battle* (Boston: Little Brown, 1961), 194.

[15] See p. 164 above.

[16] On this point, the following comment of Eric Voegelin is worth attention: "We are confronted with the singular situation that Christian faith is so much the more threatened, the further it expands socially, the more it brings men under institutional control and the more clearly its essence is articulated. This threat had reached the critical point in the high Middle Ages because of widespread social success. Christianity had in fact institutionally encompassed the men of Western society; and in the new urban culture, under the influence of the great religious orders, its essence had attained a high degree of clarity. Coincidentally with its greatness, a weakness became apparent: great masses of Christianized men who were not strong enough for

that this doctrine can be true, can be the correct statement of common human destiny.

And yet if we examine what the modern world is, at its core, if we look at what modern science, in its research, often projects, we find a persistent effort to create for us an alternative to, or even a parody of, the eternal life that is outlined or hinted at in the revelational tradition. What is then proposed is a life in this world that purportedly offers the same things—no death, full health, no strife—that the doctrine of eternal life offers to believers.[17] Only now the project is said to be "realistic", not "mythological" or ideological, as the Christian revelation's description and anticipation are said to be.

Benedict XVI carefully dealt with this alternative in *Spe Salvi* and other writings.[18] It has long been a truism in political philosophy, ever since perhaps Bury's famous book on progress, that the energy of modern social movements comes largely from an abidingly secularized Christian zeal for an end that has been relocated from the next world to this one.[19] The "lowering of our sights" from the next world to this one, said to have been the effect of Machiavelli, managed,

---

the heroic adventure of faith became susceptible to ideas that could give them a greater degree of certainty about the meaning of their existence than faith. The reality of being as it is known in its truth in Christianity is difficult to bear, and the flight from clearly seen reality to Gnostic constructions will probably always be a phenomenon of wide extent in civilizations that Christianity has permeated." *Science, Politics, and Gnosticism* (Chicago: Regnery, 1968), 109.

[17] See James V. Schall, *The Modern Age* (South Bend, Ind.: St. Augustine's Press, 2010).

[18] See especially Joseph Ratzinger [Benedict XVI], *Eschatology: Death and Eternal Life* (Washington, D.C.: Catholic University of America Press, 1988).

[19] J. B. Bury, *The Idea of Progress: Its Origin and Growth* (New York: Macmillan, 1932).

along with German philosophy, to incorporate evil into the "modern project" without eliminating the claim, in the words of Francis Bacon, "to improve the human estate".[20] Evil became, indeed, itself an agent of this good, to be used, not avoided, at the cost of the transcendent end itself.

Most modern ideologies are little more than efforts to bring the Kingdom of God to this earth by some sort of human means. Philosophically, this same effort, itself properly located by Augustine in the *City of God*, is often a continuation of the classical Platonic issue of the proper location of the "city in speech" that Socrates sketched from book 2 on in the *Republic*. From these revelational or Platonic origins, most of the ideologies take their mandate to change the world so that it will be perfect not in the hereafter but in the here and now. It is to be the product not of grace or God but of human enterprise or genius, the real work of the "practical sciences".

The ideologies differ not so much in their end as in their analysis of the means to attain the end—revolutionary, economic, political, biological, or, probably in the case of Islam, religious. The German philosopher Eric Voegelin, as we will see in a moment, calls such endeavors "gnostic" (mind formulated) because they are projections of the autonomous human mind onto reality, not the human mind learning from an already existing reality what man and the world are about.

Voegelin has been particularly insightful in tracing and elaborating this process of transforming Christian transcendent goals into this-worldly enterprises. Voegelin, in fact, argues that it is precisely the weakness of faith in Christian men that tempts them to doubt the truth of the supernatural

---

[20] See Leo Strauss, *Thoughts on Machiavelli* (Glencoe, Ill.: Free Press, 1959).

order. The result is not that they forget such goals but that they open themselves to the notion that the same ends can be achieved by various economic, political, or scientific—especially, more recently, biological—means.[21]

"All gnostic movements", Voegelin wrote, "are involved in the project of absolutizing the constitution of being, and replacing it with a world-immanent order of being, the perfection of which lies in the realm of human action. This is a matter of so altering the structure of the world, which is perceived as inadequate, that a new, satisfying world arises."[22] Christian revelation places the achievement of man's end also in his own moral and intellectual life, in his own will. This center requires belief, repentance, and forgiveness.

Modern thought places the problem of unhappiness in man's very being, said in Genesis to be good but now seen to be defective. Its solution is not faith, charity, and virtue but a reconstruction of the very physical and mental structure of man himself. Self-salvation is proposed to replace redemption in Christ. The former probably could not be proposed had the latter not taken place in the form it did, in which the redeemer was true man as well as true God.

What Voegelin is saying, then, is that modern man intends to eliminate the order of nature and the transcendence that is found in reason and revelation. Man will replace eternal life with his own practice, his own concept of man in particular.[23] This *what-it-is-to-be-a-man* is no longer contemplative

---

[21] See Voegelin, *Science, Politics, and Gnosticism.*

[22] Ibid., 99–100. See David Walsh, *Modern Philosophic Revolution* (Cambridge: Cambridge University Press, 2008).

[23] Screwtape gives similar advice: "So inveterate is their [human beings'] appetite for Heaven, that our [the devils'] best method, at this stage, of attaching them to Earth is to make them believe that Earth can be turned into Heaven at some future date by politics or eugenics or 'science' or psychology

or a result of creation. It is constructive or practical. Nature, it is said, is opaque. It yields no knowledge of what man is. It is only a collection of parts to be manipulated as we choose. Literally, this new modern man, as he promises, intends to achieve the ends of a fully happy and a perhaps unending mortal life by means of his own science and technology, the extended use of his hands and brain.

This mission or enterprise, conceived also as a way of eliminating the evils associated with revelation's or religion's claim to truth, is proposed in defiance of the order of creation and redemption that is found in the classical philosophers and Scripture.[24] Voegelin calls this project—something Benedict XVI also refers to in *Spe Salvi*[25]—the "immanentization of the *eschaton*". What this rather awesome-sounding phrase means is simply that the four last things (*eschaton*)—heaven, hell, purgatory, and death—will be solved but in man's own way. He will improve on the gods. We need not wait till death and judgment; we can solve these issues by ourselves in this world. Indeed, we take up this enterprise precisely in defiance of the revelational tradition, which teaches us to achieve these ends by sacrifice, intelligence, virtue, and suffering.

Of course, such claims to refashion the world by our own powers are extraordinary. They are, however, a fair general description of the ideas that lie behind the utopian impulses of modernity. Implicitly, they mean that eternal

---

or what not. Real worldliness is a work of time—assisted, of course, by pride, for we teach them to describe the creeping death as Good Sense or Maturity or Experience." C. S. Lewis, *The Screwtape Letters* (New York: Macmillan, 1961), 133.

[24] See James V. Schall, *The Order of Things* (San Francisco: Ignatius Press, 2007).

[25] Benedict XVI, *Spe Salvi*, 23, 30, 35.

life is not the association of each human person within the inner life of the Trinity but is the "construction" of an autonomous happiness that owes nothing to the gods, Trinitarian or otherwise; all is owed to man. The human community or collectivity is imagined to replace, in ever ongoing time, the community of the Trinity in eternity. Modern community or society theories often hover over the notion of a "mortal God", to use Hobbes' term. It is the perfect and complete "humanism" that locks man into himself as the only real being in existence.

The well-known medical philosopher Edmund Pellegrino, in a lecture I once heard him deliver, said that the purpose of modern medicine, both on its speculative and practical side, is to "keep us alive forever". Naturally, this speculation flows over into practice. We see efforts to extend our lives several hundred years. Cloning and the production of bodies for "spare parts" to keep us going are designed to keep us alive beyond our threescore years and ten. This is why Voegelin, speaking of the project of modernizing, remarked that its thrust lies "in the realm of human action".

In the Greek tradition, human action is directed immediately to politics, art, and morals but indirectly to the contemplative life, as we have previously seen. Disorder in the active life generally obscures or suppresses any attention to the contemplative life. This effort to define human happiness is really the meaning of the first book of Aristotle's *Ethics*. It is contemplation, not action, however, that preserves the human and his transcendent end or goal implicit in human nature. This end is finally nothing less than the vision of the triune God, into which human beings are invited to live a life now seen as eternal.

The reason that contemplation can do this preservation is that it already knows *what man is*. He does not become some other kind of being with another end throughout the course of history. The first men had the same goal as we do. But if we eliminate God and the truths of being that He guarantees, we are left with our own practical intellect, the artistic intellect that serves as the only source of intelligence in the world. Nothing is left to check it, as no understanding of man can be found unless he is a stable being created by God to be this kind of being, not that, not subject to our powers to make him otherwise.

What are some of the indications that these "last things" are now becoming projects of human science and endeavor? With regard to hell, it can well be argued that modern totalitarian movements in their almost unlimited extremism to produce a perfect order have, in fact, produced many hells on earth. The gulags and concentration camps are gory examples.

The efforts to extend life indefinitely, to postpone death, as I have just mentioned, clearly imitate the resurrection, which in fact proposes that a particular individual will live forever, not just a species or a type. The notion of cloning so that the same corpus stays in existence down the ages is another hint at resurrection, not unlike the old notion of the soul coming back in different forms down the ages, as in reincarnation theory. Efforts to deep-freeze human bodies after death so that, when science learns how to cure the illness that caused the death, the body can be revived with the help of new technology or medicine is another imitation of immortality and resurrection.

The begetting or reproduction of individuals of any species has long been thought of as the way to keep that species in existence for a period longer than the life of an individual of the species. Indeed, it was intended to keep the species as such in existence down the ages. In the case of human beings, we have the added concern about the immortality of the individual soul of each member of the human species. Many technical begetting procedures today bypass the normal sexual relation of husband and wife in which the child born to them is known to be theirs and is begotten in their love. This newer system puts human beings into the world with unidentified or unacknowledged origins, the responsibility for whom is difficult to establish. We in fact see a general decline in that confidence and vigor by which human populations in the nations are sustained. The decline and elimination of many peoples and nations are now the results of violations of the basic understanding of what human begetting is for, both in this life and the next.

The ironic point of these considerations is that, though seeking ends implicit in human nature, they end up with aberrant forms that undermine it. In every case, the classical position is superior to what is said to replace it. The alternative earthly paradise in this world turns out in practice to be closer to hell than heaven. The postponement of death usually is just that, a postponement after ever-increasing efforts and suffering. The efforts to keep individuals alive interfere with their replacement by normal births in subsequent generations. Homosexuality, sexual "freedom", and related moral disorders result in fewer births and in more disordered personal lives of the citizens.

The arguments in favor of classical morality are best made when contrasted to the alternatives that are proposed to replace them. The effort to replace eternal life by some inner-worldly, ongoing paradise, the real impulse behind much modern thought and science, does not work. Christian thinking remains superior to what is proposed to replace it. This fact should strike us as strange, although when reflected on, it is but another "reasonable pleasure". It does indicate an intelligence in things that is not simply there of our own or its own making, an intelligence that evidently looks out for us better than we do.

Perhaps the most graphic consideration with regard to eternal life, one indicated throughout these pages, is that it is not achieved apart from each individual person's own freedom and willingness to receive it. It is true that we, each of us, shall all live forever, whether we choose it or not. This consequence is the meaning of the immortality of the soul, of the Last Judgment, and of the resurrection of the body. No final alternative to heaven or hell exists.

Purgatory is, as Benedict XVI also says in *Spe Salvi*, both reasonable and temporary.[26] But its understanding flows logically from its premise, the need to be fully prepared to know and see God. This preparation is something operative both from the divine side and from the human side. In that sense, purgatory is something we want when we understand the nature and heinousness of our own sins. We might empirically doubt its reality, but its logic seems inescapable. We do not want to see God if we are not ready to do so.

IV

The whole of the Christian understanding thus can be summed in this way. The triune God is a complete and everlasting communion of the three Persons—Father, Son, and Spirit—in one substance or nature. This divinity needs nothing outside of itself. The whole Trinity freely created outside of itself other rational beings who are not gods.

[26] Benedict XVI, *Spe Salvi*, 25.

The rest of the cosmos is created in the light of the end of the rational creatures within it. The mortal persons who do or have existed, that is, we ourselves, were, and always remain, each individually, finite persons.

We are invited, however, each of us, to lead "rational" lives according to our level of being. In addition, and our actual being is ordered to it, we were given and offered the inner life of the Godhead as our end. Each human person is invited—and this is the meaning of the course of our lives, no matter when or where lived—personally to accept it. All of us are also given the grace to receive and participate in this higher life after our own manner.[27] This participation and the drama of its selection are essentially what the universe is about. This working out of the salvation of human persons is the most important thing happening in our universe. All else is its background and stage.

The universe and the earthly cities within it provide a place, an arena, for this divine plan to be carried out in the lives and wills of existing human persons while they pass through their lives in actual cities. The divine invitation is played out against the mortal lives of human persons in their thoughts and actions, "what they have done or what they have failed to do".[28] Through virtue and vice, through the love or hatred of their God and neighbor, they decide in thought and practice whether they will

[27] "A recurring theme in these publications [of Benedict XVI] is the idea that Christianity is primarily about a person's participation in the life and love of the Trinity, mediated through the sacraments, especially the Eucharist. For Benedict, the reduction of Christianity to the status of an ethical code is an impoverished representation of true Christianity." Tracey Rowland, "Ratzinger the Rift Healer", *Record*, October 29, 2010, http://www.therecord.com.au/blog/dr-tracey-rowland-ratzinger-the-rift-healer/.

[28] Cf. the penitential rite of the Mass.

accept the invitation to complete their lives in eternal life itself or whether they will reject it. They can indeed reject this offer. Evidently, not a few do, as many passages in Scripture seem to imply.

Those who finally make this rejection of God, in effect, select themselves as the center of existence for eternity. They repeat the sin of the angels and of Adam and Eve in their own souls. If it were not possible to reject God by choosing oneself, it would not be possible to love Him either. This love is the very reality of the inner life of the Trinity that is offered to us. It is precisely because the Good for which we are created is so exalted that we cannot possess it unless we choose to accept it. The love that is God can only be given and received in freedom if it is to mean anything either to God or to us.

Those who accept what is the purpose of their creation in the first place, in effect, choose to enter the Kingdom of God, as it is called. They do not freely close themselves off from the rest of creation. This latter path of not isolating the self is what God intended for each human person from the beginning. Short of denying men's freedom, God made every necessary provision in grace and providence for them to accept the divine invitation. They ultimately enter and live this eternal life as complete human persons, body and soul, with their complete human record manifested.

At the resurrection of the body, the whole person is again completely restored and elevated. It can now receive what it has been promised. Human happiness belongs to these resurrected persons—they see and love God "face to face", as Saint Paul put it (1 Cor 13:12)—and is enhanced by other beings, generally known as the communion of saints. These are they who have accepted and dwell in the same end, the same eternal and Trinitarian life.

The mechanism, so to speak, by which this final status of each person is worked out is what is called "the judgment". In the Nicene Creed, we read that Christ will come "to judge the living and the dead". Such judgment, the Last Judgment, is often, as in the Sistine Chapel or in Dante, pictured in awesome terms, no doubt rightly so. But essentially, its necessity and nature are intelligible to us in general outline. Yet "everything created by God is good, and nothing is to be rejected if it is received with thanksgiving; for then it is consecrated by the word of God and prayer", Paul told Timothy (1 Tim 4:4–5). The judgment is not about what God has made. What God has made is already good. It is about what man has chosen in his freedom. Man's ultimate good requires his freely choosing his own goodness.

If we return to Plato's concern about whether the world was or was not created in justice, we really can see what must happen and what is at stake. It is indeed the great rational pleasure to understand the judgment, that it is just. Blessed John Paul II had said in *Memory and Identity* that the limits of evil are found in the mercy of God.[29] God's justice is seen in the light of His mercy, in the light of the forgiveness of sins. God does not eliminate the possibility of sin, but He does forgive sins, if the sinner asks and repents. This too is central to the drama of ongoing human existence. But evidently not all things can be forgiven. Among these things that cannot be forgiven, because it wills not to be, is the preference of oneself over all other goods, especially the highest ones.

Eternal life is thus the completion or end of one step in our lives and the beginning. It begins with death and the judgment that manifests how well we have lived not by our

---

[29] John Paul II, *Memory and Identity* (New York: Rizzoli, 2005), 166ff.

own criterion but by that of the Lord who made us. The final rational pleasure is to comprehend that the unsettlement we find in our souls over the insufficiency of all finite things was no accident. We were simply made so that nothing less than seeing God, in His inner life, face-to-face, would satisfy us.

The long history of the human race and of each of our lives within it testifies to the same thing. We are made for eternal life, not for anything that we ourselves might substitute for it. The whole of modernity has been little more than man's desperate effort to find another end for himself than the one given to him by God as the real end of his desiring. We find a contentment in this realization that none of our ideas are what we really want. With this understanding, we can relax and enjoy the world as it is given to us, hazardous as it often is. We do not have to formulate a new man to replace the one we are given at conception and birth.

We need rather to understand that we have been given far more than we deserve or could hope for. God does not violate our freedom, but He does worry about our intelligence when we choose something so much less than what we truly want if we could but grasp its wonder. This is why we must end where we began, that the real temptation against the truth of Christianity is not that we have been given too little but that we have been given too much. In this sense, the characteristic of our worship and of our minds is simply awe, simply the utter astonishment that such things really are and that they are given to us.

CONCLUSION

ONE WHIRLING ADVENTURE:
THE STRANGE COHERENCES
OF CATHOLICISM

Who could plumb the un-plumbable depth of God's counsel and scrutinize his inscrutable design? This is the design
by which God made man as a being in time, when no man
had existed before him, making him in time with no change
of purpose, and multiplying the whole human race from
that one man.

—Augustine, *City of God*[1]

Happiness for individual persons or for a people is something given rather than something pursued. We really do
not know what we want or what is good for us. It may be
that the worst things—the loss of the best things, the loss
of everything—are for the best. Had not Troy fallen, there
could have been no Rome.

—Dennis Quinn, *Iris Exiled: A Synoptic History of Wonder*[2]

To have fallen into any one of the fads from Gnosticism to
Christian Science would indeed have been obvious and tame.
But to have avoided them all has been *one whirling adven-
ture*; and in my vision the heavenly chariot flies thundering

[1] Augustine, *City of God*, trans. Henry Bettenson (Harmondsworth, England:
Penguin, 2003), 12.15.
[2] Dennis Quinn, *Iris Exiled: A Synoptic History of Wonder* (Lanham, Md.:
University Press of America, 2002), 109.

through the ages, the dull heresies sprawling and prostrate, the wild truth reeling but erect.

— G. K. Chesterton, *Orthodoxy*[3]

I

The title of this book, to recall it again as we conclude, is *Reasonable Pleasures*. It is, as I said, an Aristotelian-inspired title with Catholic overtones. Aristotle, while acknowledging pleasure as a good, was careful not to define or identify happiness as such with pleasure. But happiness did not exclude the reality of pleasure either. Nonetheless, he spent a good deal of time on the meaning and diversity of our pleasures. They are often considered to be major obstacles to a noble life and causes of a dissolute one. Frequently enough, they are such obstacles and causes.

But we take care to see exactly why pleasure is problematic. It is a worthy reflection to understand it properly. Common sense and experience alert us to the ways pleasure can obscure our goals. The dangers that arise from pleasure are the frequent subject matter of the moralists and spiritual teachers from almost all religions and philosophical persuasions. Even the hedonists and epicureans strive to put it in place. Something of its often ambiguous presence is found in most novels and poetry. This danger must be acknowledged, but with caution, lest pleasure as such be seen as an evil, a perennial temptation that is also to be rejected.

---

[3] G. K. Chesterton, *Orthodoxy* in *Collected Works*, vol. 1 (San Francisco: Ignatius Press, 1986), 306 (emphasis added).

Aristotle's treatise on the virtues in his *Ethics* is little more than a guide to keep pleasure disciplined between "too much" and "too little". A Stoic apathy or a Kantian duty ethic seems rigorous, even lofty. They are aware of the impurity that might come into our motivations from pleasure's influence. They want to exclude pleasure as such, however, something quite contrary to the sensible Aristotle, who understands its proper place.

Yet to act as if pleasure did not exist or as if it were not itself good and usually helpful is inhuman and unreasonable. Certainly nothing is found in Catholicism that would have a problem with this basic Aristotelian outlook on the valuable but subordinate role of pleasure in human life. Christ knew about the lilies of the field, the wine at Cana, and the loaves and the fishes, as well as the dangers that arise from mammon and pride. In any sane understanding of *what is*, both the good and the danger associated with pleasure need to be kept present and in balance.

Thus, in this book, we have pointedly referred to "reasonable pleasures", not just pleasures, though the experience of *what pleasure is* will be pretty much the same when pleasure is used well or ill. If pleasure automatically ceased when it was wrongly used, we would not be tempted to separate the pleasure from the act in which it properly belongs and obtains its morality. Evil arises from how we will, not from what is itself good, as even the will as a faculty is. The right or wrong of any pleasure does not consist in the pleasure itself, which, as such, is always good. We are not Manicheans who find anything connected with matter or the body, especially pleasure, to be evil. The right and wrong come from how we will the end, from the end and circumstances of the activity in which a proper pleasure exists.

Pleasure seems to be designed to enhance the goodness of the act in which it exists. Something superabundant hovers about it, almost as if to say that we always find more to reality than what is minimally needed just to exist. As Chesterton said: "Blessed is he who expecteth nothing, for he shall be gloriously surprised." [4] We wonder about this phenomenon also. Aristotle called pleasure a kind of "bloom" on an action. [5]

But since we can in action and thought, at least, separate the pleasure from the proper action in which it exists, we can elevate pleasure to our end. If, by the power of our will, we make this separation, causing the pleasure to be our real end, we still must face the consequences of the act itself in which the pleasure was found, what it was about. The action continues to lack the good that was due to it, even if the pleasure is present. The evil or good consequences follow the act, not the pleasure that is present in the act.

Often in these chapters, I have pointed out sundry "rational pleasures" that are found in human activities. Indeed, I have stressed the fact that our mind, in the very activity of its knowing or thinking, has its own particular pleasure, quite unlike other pleasures that we also have. A particularly satisfying pleasure is found in just knowing, knowing the truth of a thing, of an action or of what is made, knowing it for its own sake.

Aristotle himself observed that if we do not locate pleasure properly, grasping the peculiar pleasure that belongs to each different activity, we will likely pursue other pleasures

---

[4] G. K. Chesterton, *Heretics*, in *Collected Works*, vol. 1 (San Francisco: Ignatius Press, 1986), 69.
[5] Aristotle, *Ethics*, 1174b34.

in a disordered manner. He noted this temptation to be particularly true of the politician. He is often too busy to experience the knowledge of the higher things that would serve to put all activities in their proper place, including his own.

The subtitle of this book, however, has not been much mentioned in the course of these pages. The omission was deliberate, but now it is time to join the two titles. The main title is *Rational Pleasures*, while the subtitle is *The Strange Coherences of Catholicism*. Things that at first do not seem to belong together, suddenly do, when reflected on. This is why Catholicism, in spite of its name, is not an "ism", not an ideology, but a description and an understanding of *what is*.

Moreover, I use the word *strange* to describe things that cohere when we do not expect or anticipate that they do. I used the word *surprised* earlier from Chesterton because surprise is one of our primary experiences not just when we learn that there are things but we see how they fit together. The connection can best be seen if we confront the reason-revelation paradox as understood in the Catholic tradition.

Briefly, the truths of revelation, while often not directly able to be proved or understood by human reason, still, when thought about, cause reason to be more, not less, reason. Reason itself belongs to reason. Thus, Aristotle did not know of the dogma of the resurrection of the body. So he did not think about it. Those who receive this doctrine, however, cannot avoid wondering about it to see whether it is at all reasonable or not. If it is totally contradictory or unreasonable, they too will have to reject it.

Nonetheless, Aristotle's correction of Plato that the human being was not just soul but soul and body, combined with the Greek idea of the immortality of the soul, made it possible to understand the Incarnation in such a way that the same person who died is the same person who rises again. This connection was a "strange coherence".

Once we come to this point of suspecting that at least some things that seem incoherent in fact are not, then we can further see that Aristotle's treatment of friendship likewise relates precisely to the doctrine of the resurrection of the body and to the eternal life of the persons who are friends. This desire for permanence is something found in every genuine love of friendship. The very notion of love means that it wishes and intends the good of the other. That good of permanence needs to be reciprocal, something belonging both to the lover and to the beloved. In a way, it is a cause of despair if we have an understanding of human life that is simply confined to this world with no opening to transcendence, to permanent things, even in the activities of our souls, in intelligence.

The "strange coherence" we finally find is just what we would want if we could have it. This completion seems to be in fact what we have and are offered, should we choose to accept it. To understand revelation, then, is to understand why we might need or might be helped by knowing Aristotle and the ferment of our reason, of our reasonable pleasures. Eugene Rogers has put the principle most concisely: "Aquinas has so arranged things that the more Aristotelian he is, the greater is the power of grace." [6]

But just to know revelation without relating it to Aristotle, to the philosopher, to philosophy would make it seem

---

[6] Eugene Rogers, "Faith and Reason Follow Glory", in *The Theology of Thomas Aquinas*, ed. R. van Nieuwenhove and J. Wawrykow (Notre Dame, Ind.: University of Notre Dame Press, 2005), 442.

that revelation is geared for some sort of being alien to ourselves. And here it is all right to be concerned with ourselves. For that is what eternal life is about. In the end, it is we who are given to know God face-to-face in that Trinitarian reality we call Father, Son, and Spirit, something that is a surprise, a gift, and the final reason why we exist at all.

We are constantly struck by the way that what is revealed to us responds to what it is that we would most want if we could have it. This awareness is the Chestertonian paradox that the greatest temptation against the faith is not that it is too fantastic or improbable but that it is too good to be true. In effect, this conclusion is the meaning of this book. That it is too good to be true, but nonetheless it is true, is also ironically the basis of any final rejection of the truth that is spelled out in Catholicism by those who choose against the light. We do not often, I know, formulate the issues in this way. Yet it is the only way to present the real coherences of Catholicism.

We are wont to stick with the "problems", with the bad record of certain clerics, for instance. We are shocked along with Nietzsche that "the last Christian died on the Cross", even though He came to save sinners who continue to abound among us. To be scandalized that Catholics or anybody else sins, or to think that sin or evil will somehow be automatically removed by some formula or movement, is completely to misunderstand the revelation of forgiveness.

We read the scholars with their presumed "proof" that Christ really did not exist but was somehow a product of a community or of what was fervently wished for. And if it were true that Christ were only a myth or a wish, we would not have to take Him seriously. Then we open Benedict XVI's work entitled *Jesus of Nazareth*. We find that it is devoted totally to the evidence that in fact Christ did exist, that He was by no means a myth. Pope Benedict XVI says exactly the same thing as did the first pope. Moreover, the best explanation of who Christ is, even scientifically, is that He was what He said He was, namely, the Son of Man, the Son of God. He showed every indication that He was such and knew that He was. Strange coherences indeed!

At the beginning of this conclusion, I cited a passage of Dennis Quinn, from his history of the idea of wonder. It is wonder, as Aristotle said, not need, not determinism, that is the primary factor in our drive to know. We want to know the truth of things, just that. And yet we do not quite know what we want, almost as if our wants are somehow not good enough for us. Whatever it is that we want will have to be given to us before we will know that we wanted it.

This status of being receivers, of being creatures who are given not only our being but also our happiness, if we choose it, constitutes any complete judgment about what we are. Aristotle had said that it seems that the gods would give us the best things if they could—happiness, as he said. It is a strange coherence in Catholicism that this is precisely what did happen. What we really want is what is given to us.

God, as Augustine said, made us to be beings in time. But we did not exist before we existed. Yet God knew us. The multiplying of the numbers of the human race throughout time did not change the reason any men were created. Estimates suggest that perhaps a hundred billion human beings have thus far existed on this planet, of whom some seven billion are alive now.

This estimate of world population numbers suggests that up to this point, some 93 percent of the human race have already decided in which final city they shall live. They also are awaiting the final judgment, whichever way they choose. It is a strange coherence that the resurrection of the body ensures that those who have been unjust and those who have been just will be identified in their choices. No room for abstraction or collective guilt is left open. All real justice and injustice is, in the final analysis, personal, attributed to someone someplace.

Plato was most concerned, as I have often noted, that the world was not made in injustice. This disordered world would be the case if crimes finally went unpunished or generous deeds unrewarded. Plato's doctrine of the immortality of the soul, while it is not wrong, is incomplete. It is not a "soul" that commits crimes or does something virtuous. Rather, it is the whole man, body and soul, acting through his own powers. In this sense, the strange coherence introduced by revelation saves Plato and his truth by completing him. So Augustine, who read Plato, as he tells us in his *Confessions*, found the Word there in the Platonists but not the Word made flesh. The whole human race is derived from one man but is also saved in time by one Man. The "inscrutable design" of God, His "un-plumbable depth", is made known to us in part, at least, as Aquinas says, that we may know something more of God Himself than we can know by our unaided reason alone.

Chesterton tells us, in a powerful image, that the "heavenly chariot flies thundering through the ages". It is battered by the untruths designed to unhinge it. These are the heresies that explain our being and destiny in such a way that we do not finally reach what is too good to be true. No human reason can be found why it is still what it is, battered though it be. The greatest of adventures is not to concoct the fads and heresies but to "whirl" past them, to line them up to see how each, in its own way, would, if followed, make us all less than we ought and want to be.

The strange coherences of Catholicism are themselves, when looked at in this light, reasonable pleasures. To know the deviations from truth or good is itself a pleasure and a good thing. This is why Catholicism, true to its Greek name, is universal, why it wants to know the heresies as well as the dogmas and doctrines. It has a thirst for reasonable pleasures. And this search is, at bottom, a search not just for a propositional understanding of truth but for the truth that lies in our being, the truth that suggests that though we are, as Saint Peter tells us, "aliens and exiles" (1 Pet 2:11), we are also created to be at home in that only place where home can finally be found, in eternal life.

Belloc, in his *Four Men*, writes: "Whatever you read in all the writings of men, and whatever you hear in all the speech of men, and whatever you notice in the eyes of men, of expression or reminiscence or desire, you will see nothing in any man's speech or writing or expression to match that which marks his hunger for home." [7] Chesterton also said that there is nothing quite so strange as this feeling we have, again and again throughout our lives, that, even when we do have a real home, we still find ourselves homesick there.

This feeling suggests that our true home includes our earthly home with all its loves. But our earthly home is itself ordered to what is more permanent, to eternal life that gives our passing lives their final meaning. This sense of a final strange coherence is the reasonable pleasure that I would leave the reader with. Though this coherence includes the whirling adventure of life and love, of the Cross and

[7] Hilaire Belloc, *The Four Men* (London: Thomas Nelson, 1912), 204.

death, of resurrection and eternal life, it is indeed "too good to be true". And that is the one solid reason, I suspect, why it just might be.

The "dull" heresies are indeed "sprawling and prostrate". The "wild truth" is "reeling" but stands "erect". The truth is called "wild" deliberately. By all "reasonable" investigations of the philosophers, ancient and modern, who have looked into these things, the truth should not be true, the coherences should not cohere. The only drawback is that things do cohere. This realization too is a rational pleasure that none of us should deny himself.

The last citation at the beginning of this book, from Aquinas, will best serve as the rational pleasure that results from such strange coherences: "The perfection of the whole of corporeal nature depends in a certain sense on the perfection of man." The perfection of man himself depends on his accepting two gifts that are also surprises, the gift of his own being and the gift of his being ordered from his beginning to live the inner life of the Trinity. To make this gift, God had to take the ultimate risk that it could be freely rejected. But to accept it, in the end, is to find the true location of our home even when we catch intimations of it in the homes in which we are born, dwell, and live our mortal lives.

SELECT BIBLIOGRAPHY

The goal of this bibliography is to illustrate and expand the central thesis of this book—namely, that things do fit together, that revelation makes sense, that revelation is addressed to reason, and that we are each ordered to a transcendent destiny, a road along that we have all already begun but that we must choose.

Arkes, Hadley. *First Things: An Inquiry into the First Principles of Morals and Justice*. Princeton, N.J.: Princeton University Press, 1985.

Benedict XVI [Joseph Ratzinger]. *Eschatology: Death and Eternal Life*. Washington, D.C.: Catholic University of America Press, 1988.

———. *Jesus of Nazareth*. Vol. 1, *From the Baptism in the Jordan to the Transfiguration*. New York: Doubleday, 2007. Vol. 2, *Holy Week: From the Entrance into Jerusalem to the Resurrection*. San Francisco: Ignatius Press, 2011. Vol. 3, *Jesus of Nazareth: Infancy Narratives*. New York: Image, 2012.

———. *Spe Salvi* [Saved in hope]. Boston: Pauline Books, 2007.

Bochenski, J.M. *Philosophy—An Introduction*. New York: Harper Torchbooks, 1972.

Brague, Rémi. *The Legend of the Middle Ages*. Chicago: University of Chicago Press, 2009.

Caldecott, Stratford. *Beauty in the Word: Rethinking the Foundations of Education*. Tacoma, Wash.: Angelico Press, 2012.

Chesterton, G. K. *Orthodoxy*. In *Collected Works*, vol. 1. San Francisco: Ignatius Press, 1986.

Gilson, Étienne. *The Unity of Philosophical Experience*. San Francisco: Ignatius Press, 1999.

Guardini, Romano. *The Humanity of Christ*. New York: Pantheon, 1964.

Huizinga, Johan. *Homo Ludens: A Study of the Play Element in Culture*. Boston: Beacon, 1950.

John Paul II. *Crossing the Threshold of Hope*. New York: Knopf, 1994.

Kass, Leon. *The Hungry Soul: Eating and the Perfection of Our Nature*. New York: Free Press, 1994.

Kreeft, Peter. *The Philosophy of Tolkien*. San Francisco: Ignatius Press, 2005.

Lewis, C. S. *The Screwtape Letters*. New York: Macmillan, 1961.

Maritain, Jacques. *Approaches to God*. New York: Collier, 1954.

Mascall, Eric. *The Christian Universe*. London: Darton, Longmans, and Todd, 1966.

Morse, Jennifer Roback. *Love and Economics*. Dallas: Spence, 2001.

Nichols, Aidan. *G. K. Chesterton, Theologian*. Manchester, N.H.: Second Spring, 2009.

Owens, Joseph. *Human Destiny: Some Problems for Catholic Philosophy*. Washington, D.C.: Catholic University of America Press, 1985.

Pieper, Josef. *In Defense of Philosophy*. San Francisco: Ignatius Press, 1992.

———. *Josef Pieper: An Anthology*. San Francisco: Ignatius Press, 1989.

Quinn, Dennis. *Iris Exiled: A Synoptic History of Wonder*. Lanham, Md.: University Press of America, 2002.

Ratzinger, Joseph. *See* Benedict XVI.

Reilly, Robert. *The Closing of the Muslim Mind.* Wilmington: ISI Books, 2010.

———. *Surprised by Beauty: A Listener's Guide to the Recovery of Modern Music.* Washington, D.C.: Morley Books, 2002.

Rowland, Tracey. *Benedict XVI: A Guide for the Perplexed.* London: T&T Clark, 2010.

Sayers, Dorothy. *The Whimsical Christian.* New York: Macmillan, 1978.

Schall, James V. *The Modern Age.* South Bend, Ind.: St. Augustine's Press, 2011.

———. *On the Unseriousness of Human Affairs.* Wilmington, Del.: ISI Books, 2001.

———. *The Order of Things.* San Francisco: Ignatius Press, 2007.

Schulz, Charles. *My Life with Charlie Brown.* Edited by M. Inge. Jackson: University Press of Mississippi, 2010.

Schumacher, E. F. *A Guide for the Perplexed.* New York: Harper Colophon, 1977.

Scruton, Roger. *The West and the Rest.* Wilmington: ISI Books, 2002.

Sokolowski, Robert. *The Phenomenology of the Human Person.* New York: Cambridge University Press, 2008.

Spitzer, Robert. *New Proofs for the Existence of God: Contributions of Contemporary Physics and Philosophy.* Grand Rapids, Mich.: Eerdmans, 2010.

Veatch, Henry. *Aristotle: A Contemporary Appreciation.* Bloomington: Indiana University Press, 1974.

Weigel, George. *The End and the Beginning: John Paul II—The Victory of Freedom, the Last Years, the Legacy.* New York: Doubleday, 2010.

Wilhelmsen, Frederick. *The Paradoxical Structure of Existence.* Albany, N.Y.: Preserving Christian Publications, 1995.

INDEX

abortion, 130
accidental occurrences, 93–94
action
   contemplation compared with,
     160–66, 182
   passion vs., 94
   pleasure separated from, 193
"acts of God", 90–91
Adam and Eve, 52, 107, 111,
   138, 140, 171, 187. *See also*
   Fall of man
Adams, John, 123, 125
Adler, Mortimer, 41–42
Adorno, Theodor, 112
After Writing: On the Liturgical
   Consummation of Philosophy
   (Pickstock), 154
agency
   of God, 92
   of man, 89–90, 91, 94, 95
Ali, Ayaan Hirsi, 105
Allah, 83, 152
Ambrose (saint), 171–72, 173
angels, fallen, 61–62
antientropic principle, 89
Apocalyptic notion of
   government, 109
Aquinas. *See* Thomas Aquinas
aristocracies, 128
Aristotle
   on action vs. passion, 94
   on evil in earthly cities, 130–31

on friendship, 195
on government, 108–9
on happiness, 182, 191, 197
on knowledge, 5, 12, 17–18,
   197
on laughter, 56
logic of, 13, 19
on man, 162, 194–95
on the mind, 12, 17
on nature, 148
Nicomachean Ethics, 5, 11, 17,
   56, 182, 192
on pain, 62
on pleasure, 12, 62, 191, 192,
   193–94
Poetics, 146
on politics and political nature
   of man, 127, 132, 134, 194
on regime classification,
   128–29
on seriousness, 146
on slavery, 161
on sports and play, 73, 75, 82,
   83, 146
athletics. *See* sports and play
Augustine (saint)
   City of God, 122, 136, 167,
   179, 190
   Confessions, 198
   on earthly cities, 122, 136, 179
   on enduring suffering, 138
   on eternal life, 167

Memory and Identity (John Paul
  II), 188
mercy. *See* forgiveness; grace;
  redemption
mind. *See also* intellect;
  knowledge
  Aristotle on, 12, 17
  Catholic Church view of,
    15–16
  Chesterton on, 33
  creation and, 17
  defense of, 24
  divinity and, 15
  dogma and, 33
  humor, role in, 55
  perfection of, 35–36
  Plato on, 14
  reality and, 32, 34
  senses and, 34
  truth and, 31, 32, 34
mirth of Christ, 58. *See also* wit
  and humor
modern ideologies, 178–82,
  183–84
monarchies, 128
monastic life, 20–21, 158, 161,
  162, 163
money spent on sports and play,
  71–72, 74
moral disorders, 184
music, Benedict XVI on, 82
My Life with Charlie Brown
  (Schulz), 48

natural disasters, 89, 90, 93
nature. *See also* cosmos; creation
  Aristotle on, 148
  grace, relationship with, 39
  laws of, 24, 26

neighbors, love for, 85, 117, 157,
  163, 186
Newman, John Henry, 30,
  143–44, 147, 164, 177
New Testament, 38, 133, 159,
  174
Nicene Creed, 35, 149, 169, 188
Nicomachean Ethics (Aristotle), 5,
  11, 17, 56, 182, 192
Nietzsche, Friedrich, 196

occasionalism, 83, 92, 152
Old Testament, 38, 105, 111,
  133, 151
oligarchies, 128
omniscience of God, 51
On the Trinity (Augustine), 6, 21
ontological materialism, 41
Order of Saint Benedict, 158,
  161
Order of Saint Dominic, 158,
  162
original sin, 131
Orthodoxy (Chesterton), 5, 18,
  58, 190–91

pain and suffering
  Aristotle on, 62
  Augustine on, 138
  bodily vs. spiritual, 62
  of Christ, 96, 140
  elimination and relief of,
    60–61
  endurance of, 138
  of evil, 67, 96–97, 100, 101
  in fallen angels, 61–62
  Paul on, 114, 160
  salvation and, 155
  spiritual pain, 62